VOLUME 3

ROME AND
THE CLASSICAL WEST

THE ILLUSTRATED
HISTORY OF THE WORLD

VOLUME 3

ROME AND
THE CLASSICAL WEST

J. M. ROBERTS

DUNCAN BAIRD PUBLISHERS

LONDON

The Illustrated History of the World

This edition first published in Great Britain in 1999

Duncan Baird Publishers
Sixth Floor
Castle House
75–76 Wells Street
London W1P 3RE

ROME AND THE CLASSICAL WEST
Copyright © Editorial Debate SA 1998
Text Copyright © J. M. Roberts 1976, 1980, 1983, 1987, 1988, 1992, 1998
Artwork and Diagrams Copyright © Editorial Debate SA 1998
(for copyright of photographs and maps, see acknowledgments on pages 191–92, which are to be regarded as an extension of this copyright)

Art Direction by Duncan Baird Publishers.
Produced by Duncan Baird Publishers, London, England, and Editorial Debate, Madrid, Spain.

British Library Cataloguing-in-Publication Data.
A catalogue record for this book is available from the British Library.

ISBN 1-900131-82-X

DBP team:
Senior editor: Joanne Levêque
Assistant editor: Georgina Harris
Senior designer: Steven Painter
Assistant designer: Anita Schnable
Picture research: Julia Ruxton
Sales fulfilment: Ian Smalley
Map artwork: Russell Bell
Decorative borders: Lorraine Harrison

Editorial Debate team:
Editors and picture researchers:
Isabel Belmonte Martínez, Feliciano Novoa Portela,
Ruth Betegón Díez, Dolores Redondo
Editorial coordination: Ana Lucía Vila

Typeset in Sabon 11/15 pt
Colour reproduction by Trescan, Madrid, Spain
Printed in Singapore by Imago Limited

NOTE
The abbreviations CE and BCE are used throughout this book:
CE Common Era (the equivalent of AD)
BCE Before Common Era (the equivalent of BC)

10 9 8 7 6 5 4 3 2 1

CONTENTS

Introduction 6

Chapter 1
Rome 8

Chapter 2
The Roman Achievement 38

Chapter 3
Jewry and the Coming of Christianity 72

Chapter 4
The Waning of the Classical West 100

Chapter 5
The Elements of a Future 150

Time chart 180

Chapters and contents 182

Series contents 184

Index 186

Acknowledgments 191

ROME AND THE
CLASSICAL WEST

For all the enterprise of the phoenicians and the early vigour of Greek colonization there, the western half of the Mediterranean basin can reasonably be judged during several centuries to have been of only marginal importance to world history. This ceased to be true because of the actions and decisions of the ruling class of what had been at first a numerically insignificant Italian people barely distinguishable from several other agglomerations of tribes and kinship groups. Barely known about by their Greek neighbours in, say, the age of Solon, they have gone down in history to be remembered as Romans, taking their name from what began as only a tiny city-state. When they became involved, much later and as the third century BCE was drawing to a close, in the affairs of Greece and the East, the Romans opened the way to a new era of world history. They forged in the next two centuries a unique institutional structure, eventually embracing the whole Hellenistic world as well as much of western Europe, making of them for the first time a single entity. The Roman Empire, as it is now remembered, was in a sense the last of the successor states of the Alexandrian world, but it embraced much more than they had ever done. Accordingly, it was to shape much more. It was, above all, to shelter the infancy of a new world religion and put political power behind it. It was to transform economic and ethnic relationships over wide areas. It was to ensure the transmission of much of the Greek classical heritage to the future. In the longest run of all, too, it was to nourish the seeds of something not to be born until long after the Roman Empire in the West had crumbled away, the civilization of Europe, which it would continue to feed not only directly through its cultural and institutional legacy, but, through example and myth, the idea of empire itself.

Set in the small valley between the Capitoline, Palatine and Esquiline hills, the Forum in the city of Rome has been the site of political, religious and commercial buildings since the 7th century BCE. The square's monumental appearance is mainly due to the work of Julius Caesar, Augustus and Tiberius. Although its basilicas, temples and triumphant arches now stand in ruins, the Forum was once the hub of the great Roman Empire.

1 *ROME*

ALL AROUND the western Mediterranean shores and across wide tracts of western Europe, the Balkans and Asia Minor, relics can still be seen of a great achievement, the empire of Rome. In some places – Rome itself, above all – they are very plentiful. The explanation why they are there is a thousand years of history. If we no longer look back on the Roman achievement as our ancestors often did, feeling dwarfed by it, we can still be puzzled and even amazed that people could do so much. Of course, the closer the scrutiny historians give to those mighty remains and the more scrupulous their sifting of the documents which explain Roman ideals and Roman practice, the more we realize that Romans were not, after all, superhuman. The grandeur that was Rome

sometimes looks more like tinsel and the virtues its publicists proclaimed sound as much like cant as do many political slogans of today. Yet when all is said and done, there remains an astonishing and solid core of creativity. In the end, Rome remade the setting of Greek civilization. Thus Romans settled the shape of the first civilization embracing all the West. This was a self-conscious achievement. Romans who looked back on it when it was later crumbling about them still felt themselves to be Romans like those who had built it up. They were, though only in the sense that they believed it. Yet that was the most important sense. For all its material impressiveness and occasional grossness, the core of the explanation of the Roman achievement was an idea, the idea of Rome itself, the

This bronze Etruscan sculpture represents a Chimaera, a mythological fire-breathing monster, which has the body and head of a lion, a serpent for a tail, and a goat's head emerging from its back. Pieces such as this demonstrate the masterly skill of the Etruscan metalworkers.

Southern Italy 509–272 BCE

In 509 BCE, according to legend, the Romans drove the last king of the Etruscan Tarquin Dynasty out of Rome and established a republican system. Roman expansion towards southern Italy began in the 5th century BCE. Rome maintained control over the neighbouring towns by allowing her "allies" the freedom of self-government, while at the same time imposing Roman foreign policy on them and forcing them to supply soldiers for the powerful Roman army.

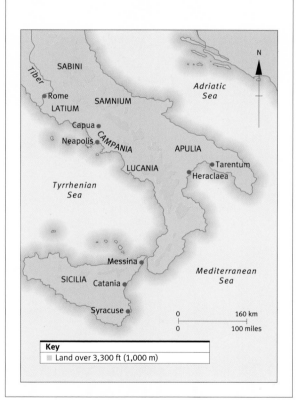

Key
- Land over 3,300 ft (1,000 m)

The Capitoline She-Wolf, a 5th-century BCE Etruscan sculpture. Legend has it that the abandoned twins Romulus and Remus were saved by a she-wolf. They went on to found the city of Rome, but Romulus killed his brother and ruled as sole king.

values it embodied and imposed, the notion of what was one day to be called *romanitas*.

It was believed to have deep roots. Romans said their city was founded by one Romulus in 753 BCE. We need not take this seriously, but the legend of the foster-mother wolf which suckled both Romulus and his twin, Remus, is worth a moment's pause; it is a good symbol of early Rome's debt to a past that was dominated by the people called Etruscans, among whose cults has been traced a special reverence for the wolf.

THE ETRUSCANS

In spite of a rich archaeological record with many inscriptions and much scholarly effort to make sense of it the Etruscans remain a mysterious people. All that has been delineated with some certainty is the general nature of Etruscan culture, not its history or chronology. Different scholars have argued that Etruscan civilization came into existence at a wide range of different times, stretching from the tenth to

Time chart (753 BCE–44 BCE)

							49–45 BCE Civil War between the armies of Caesar and Pompey
		509 BCE Establishment of the Roman Republic		264–241 BCE First Punic War		149–146 BCE Third Punic War	
700 BCE	600 BCE	500 BCE	400 BCE	300 BCE	200 BCE	100 BCE	0
753 BCE Foundation of Rome, according to legend		C.450 BCE Law of the Twelve Tables		218–201 BCE Second Punic War		88–82 BCE Civil War between the armies of Marius and Sulla	44 BCE Assassination of Julius Caesar

The lifestyle and beliefs of the Etruscans

Little is known about the origins of the Etruscan people, although many historians now believe that they came from the Villanovan culture, which developed in the Po valley, and that they were also strongly influenced by ancient Greek culture. Etruscan civilization reached its peak during the 7th and 6th centuries BCE, when the Etruscans controlled a region that encompassed most of central Italy, including Rome, extending to the north as far as the Po, and to the south as far as Campania. They maintained strong trade links with Greece, based mainly on the exportation of metals, which added to the prosperity of the noble families who inhabited the Etruscan cities to the north of the Tiber.

It seems, from the opulence of the large private tombs they built on the outskirts of their cities, that the Etruscans believed in the existence of life after death. They filled their tombs with furniture and fabrics, weapons and cooking utensils – objects that, together with a number of well-preserved tomb frescoes, tell us a great deal about certain aspects of their lives and culture. It appears that the Etruscans thought their world to be ordered and regulated by the gods. Communication between the gods and human beings was believed to take place through omens. These were then interpreted by seers, whose powers of divination meant that they played an important role in Etruscan society.

Both sides of this gold tablet bear Etruscan inscriptions and abbreviated versions in Phoenician. The tablet originates from the Etruscan port of Pyrgi and probably dates from the early 5th century BCE. It forms part of a treaty between Rome and Carthage, which was signed during the first year of the republic, confirming the relationship that had been established when Rome was an Etruscan city.

A married couple, probably the master and mistress of a large household, is depicted on the lid of a 6th-century BCE sarcophagus discovered in the Etruscan burial ground at Cerveteri. The husband and wife, shown reclining on a low couch, are guests at a banquet. Unlike the Greeks, the Etruscans did not forbid women from attending such feasts.

Several colourful tomb murals have been found in the Etruscan burial ground at Tarquinia. This scene depicts servants and musicians, probably at a banquet, and is thought to date from the first half of the 5th century BCE.

the seventh century BCE. Nor have they been able to agree about where the Etruscans came from; one hypothesis points to immigrants from Asia just after the end of the Hittite Empire, but several other possibilities have their supporters. All that is obvious is that they were not the first Italians. Whenever they came to the peninsula and wherever from, Italy was then already a confusion of peoples.

There were probably still at that time some aboriginal natives among them whose ancestors had been joined by Indo-European invaders in the second millennium BCE. In the next thousand years some of these Italians developed advanced cultures. Iron-working was going on in about 1000 BCE. The Etruscans probably adopted the skill from the peoples there before them, possibly from a culture which has been called Villanovan (after an archaeological site near modern Bologna). They brought metallurgy to a high

level and vigorously exploited the iron deposits of Elba, off the coast of Etruria. With iron weapons, they appear to have established an Etruscan hegemony which at its greatest extent covered the whole central peninsula, from the valley of the Po down to Campania. Its organization remains obscure, but Etruria was probably a loose league of cities governed by kings. The Etruscans were literate, using an alphabet derived from Greek which may have been acquired from the cities of Magna Graecia (though little of their writing can be understood at present), and they were relatively rich.

THE ROMAN REPUBLIC

IN THE SIXTH CENTURY BCE the Etruscans were installed in an important bridgehead on the south bank of the River Tiber. This was the site of Rome, one of a number of small cities of the Latins, an old-established people of the Campania. Through this city something of the Etruscan legacy was to survive to flow into and eventually be lost in the European tradition. Near the end of the sixth century BCE Rome broke away from Etruscan dominion during a revolt of the Latin cities against their masters. Until then, the city had been ruled by kings, the last of whom, tradition later said, was expelled in 509 BCE. Whatever the exact date, this was certainly about the time at which Etruscan power, over-strained by struggle with the western Greeks, was successfully challenged by the Latin peoples, who thereafter went their own ways.

The Romans imitated the Greek custom of erecting statues in honour of their leaders in public spaces and dedicating votive statues to them in the sanctuaries. This bronze bust of the Roman aristocrat Brutus dates from the end of the 4th century BCE.

Nevertheless, Rome was to retain much from her Etruscan past. Through it she had first had access to the Greek civilization with which she continued to live in contact both by land and sea. Rome was a focus of important land and water routes, high enough up the Tiber for her to bridge it, but not so high that she could not be reached by sea-going vessels. Fertilization by Greek influence was perhaps her most important inheritance, but Rome also carried forward many Etruscan institutions. One was the way she organized her people in "centuries" for military purposes; more superficial but striking instances were her gladiatorial games, civic triumphs and reading of auguries – a consultation of the entrails of sacrifices in order to discern the shape of the future.

EARLY REPUBLICAN GOVERNMENT

The republic was to last for more than four hundred and fifty years and even after that its institutions survived in name. Romans always harped on continuity and their loyal adherence (or reprehensible non-adherence) to the good old ways of the early republic. There was some reality in such claims, much as there is, for example, in the claims made for the continuity of parliamentary government in Great Britain or for the wisdom of the founding fathers of the United States in agreeing a constitution which still operates successfully. Yet, of course, great changes took place as the centuries passed. They eroded the institutional and ideological continuities and historians still argue about how to interpret them. Yet for all these changes Rome's institutions made possible a Roman Mediterranean and a Roman empire stretching far beyond it which was to be the cradle of Europe and Christianity. Thus Rome, like Greece (which reached many later peoples only through Rome), shaped much of the modern world. It is not just in a physical sense that we still live among her ruins.

THE CHANGING REPUBLIC

Broadly speaking the changes of republican times were symptoms and results of two main processes. One was of decay; gradually the republic's institutions ceased to work. They

Roman civilization was greatly influenced by the Greek example and it is through Rome that much of what we know about Greek culture has been preserved. This statue of Hermes with the infant Dionysus is believed to be a Roman copy of a piece by the 4th-century BCE Greek sculptor Praxiteles. The Romans copied large numbers of Greek statues.

could no longer contain political and social realities and, in the end, this destroyed them, even when their names survived. The other was the extension of Roman rule first beyond the city and then beyond Italy. For two centuries both processes went on rather slowly.

Internal politics were rooted in arrangements originally meant to make impossible the return of monarchy. Constitutional theory was concisely expressed in the motto carried by the monuments and standards of Rome until well into imperial times: SPQR, the abbreviation of the Latin words for "the Roman Senate and People". Theoretically, ultimate sovereignty always rested with the people, which acted through a complicated set of assemblies attended by all citizens in person (of course, not all inhabitants of Rome were citizens). This was similar to what went on in many Greek city-states. The general conduct of business was the concern of the Senate; it made laws and regulated the work of elected magistrates. It was in the form of tensions between the poles of Senate and people that the most important political issues of Roman history were usually expressed.

OLIGARCHY AT WORK

Rather surprisingly, the internal struggles of the early republic seem to have been comparatively bloodless. Their sequence is complicated and sometimes mysterious, but their general result was that they gave the citizen body as a whole a greater say in the affairs of the republic. The Senate, which concentrated political leadership, had come by 300 BCE or so to represent a ruling class which was an amalgamation of the old patricians of pre-republican days with the wealthier members of the *plebs*, as the rest of the citizens were termed. The Senate's members constituted an oligarchy, self-renewing though some were usually excluded in each census (which took place once every five years). Its core was a group of noble families whose origins might be plebeian, but among whose ancestors were men who had held the office of consul, the highest of the magistracies.

Two consuls had replaced the last of the kings at the end of the sixth century BCE. Appointed for a year, they ruled the state through the Senate and were its most important officers. They were bound to be men of experience and weight, for they had to have passed through at least two subordinate levels of elected office, as *quaestores* and *praetores*, before they were eligible. The *quaestores* (of whom there

The Curia Julia, the building that once housed the Senate's meeting room, can be seen in the foreground of this picture of the Roman Forum. There was originally an altar outside the entrance, at which members of the Senate offered sacrifices to the gods. At the beginning of the 4th century CE the Curia Julia was rebuilt by Diocletian.

were twenty elected each year) also automatically became members of the Senate. These arrangements gave the Roman ruling élite great cohesiveness and competence; for progress to the highest office was a matter of selection from a field of candidates who had been well tested and trained in office. That this constitution worked well for a long time is indisputable. Rome was never short of able men. What it masked was the natural tendency of oligarchy to decay into faction, for whatever victories were won by the plebs, the working of the system ensured that it was the rich who ruled and the rich who disputed the right to office among themselves. Even in the electoral college which was supposed to represent the whole people, the *comitia centuriata*, organization gave an undue proportion of influence to the wealthy.

SOCIAL FOUNDATIONS

PLEBS IS A MISLEADINGLY simple term. The word stood for different social realities at different times. Conquest and enfranchisement slowly extended the boundaries of citizenship. Even in early times they ran well beyond the city and its environs as other cities were incorporated in the republic. At that time, the typical citizen was a countryman. The basis of Roman society was always agricultural and rural. It is significant that the Latin word for money, *pecunia*, is derived from the word for a flock of sheep or herd of cattle, and that the Roman measure of land was the *iugerum*, the extent that could be ploughed in a day by two oxen. Land and the society it supported were related in changing ways during the republic, but always its base was the rural population. The later preponderance in popular memory of the image of imperial Rome, the great parasitic city, obscures this.

THE CITIZEN CLASS

The free citizens who made up the bulk of the population of the early republic were peasants, some much poorer than others. They were legally grouped in complicated arrangements whose roots were sunk in the Etruscan past. Such distinctions were economically insignificant, though they had constitutional importance for electoral purposes, and tell us less about the social realities of republican Rome than distinctions made by the Roman census between those able to equip themselves with the arms and armour needed to

The Rostrum was the platform from which political speakers addressed the Roman public in the Forum. Its name comes from the prows, or *rostra*, of six ships (captured in the war against the Latins in 338 BCE) which adorned the front section.

This funerary bas-relief, which dates from the 1st century CE, depicts a scene from the grape harvest – a very important moment in the Roman agricultural year. Workers are shown here treading grapes to extract the juice from which wine was produced.

serve as soldiers, those whose only contribution to the state was to breed children (the *proletarii*) and those who were simply counted as heads, because they neither owned property nor had families. Below them all, of course, were the slaves.

There was a persistent tendency, accelerating rapidly in the third and second centuries BCE, for many of the *plebs* who in earlier days had preserved some independence through possession of their own land to sink into poverty. Meanwhile, the new aristocracy increased its relative share of land as conquest brought it new wealth. This was a long-drawn-out process, and while it went on, new

This Roman floor mosaic shows the use of oxen and horses in the harvesting and threshing of wheat. A country villa is depicted in the background.

subdivisions of social interest and political weight appeared. Furthermore, to add another complicating factor, there grew up the practice of granting citizenship to Rome's allies. The republic in fact saw a gradual enlargement of the citizen class but a real diminution of its power to affect events.

THE PLEBEIANS

The decrease of the influence of the citizen class did not only occur because wealth came to count for so much in Roman politics. It was also because everything had to be done at Rome, though there were no representative arrangements which could effectively reflect the wishes of even those Roman citizens who lived in the swollen city, let alone those scattered all over Italy. What tended to happen instead was that threats to refuse military service or to withdraw altogether from Rome and found a city elsewhere enabled the *plebs* to restrict somewhat the powers of the Senate and magistrates. After 366 BCE, too, one of the two consuls had to be a plebeian and in 287 BCE the decisions of the plebeian assembly were given overriding force of law. But the main restriction on the traditional rulers lay in the ten elected Tribunes of the People, officers chosen by popular vote, who could initiate legislation or veto it (one veto was enough) and were available night and day to citizens who felt themselves unjustly treated by a magistrate. The tribunes had most weight when there was great social feeling or personal division in the Senate, for then they were courted by the politicians. In the earlier republic and often thereafter, the tribunes, who were members of the ruling class and might be nobles, worked for the most part easily enough with the consuls and the rest of the Senate. The administrative talent and experience of this body and the enhancement

of its prestige because of its leadership in war and emergency could hardly be undermined until there were social changes grave enough to threaten the downfall of the republic itself.

THE CONSTITUTION

The constitutional arrangements of the early republic were thus complicated, but effective. They prevented violent revolution and permitted gradual change. Yet they would be no more important to us than those of Thebes or Syracuse, had they not made possible and presided over the first phase of victorious expansion of Roman power. The story of the republic's institutions is important for even later periods, too, because of what the republic itself became. Almost the whole of the fifth century BCE was taken up in mastering Rome's neighbours and her territory was doubled in the process. The other cities of the Latin League were next subordinated; when some of them revolted in the middle of the fourth century they were forced back into it

on harsher terms. It was a little like a land version of the Athenian Empire a hundred years before; Roman policy was to leave her "allies" to govern themselves, but they had to subscribe to Roman foreign policy and supply contingents to the Roman army. In addition, Roman policy favoured established dominant groups in the other Italian communities, and Roman aristocratic families multiplied their personal ties with them. The citizens of those communities were also admitted to rights of citizenship if they migrated to Rome. Etruscan hegemony in central Italy, the richest and most developed part of the peninsula, was thus replaced by Roman.

THE EXPANSION OF ROMAN POWER

ROMAN MILITARY POWER GREW, as did the number of subjected states. The republic's own army was based on conscription. Every male citizen who owned property was obliged to serve if called, and the obligation

A small bronze statue of a 4th-century BCE Samnite warrior. He is wearing armour and would also have held a shield and a spear. The southern Italian Samnite people continued to oppose the Romans for almost three centuries after their defeat.

was heavy, sixteen years for an infantryman and ten for cavalry. The army was organized in legions of 5,000 which fought at first in solid phalanxes with long pike-like spears. It not only subdued Rome's neighbours, but also beat off a series of fourth-century incursions by Gauls from the north, though on one occasion they sacked Rome itself (390 BCE). The last struggles of this formative period came at the end of the fourth century when the Romans conquered the Samnite peoples of the Abruzzi. Effectively, the republic could now tap allied manpower from the whole of central Italy.

Rome was now at last face to face with the western Greek cities. Syracuse was by far the most important of them. Early in the third century the Greeks asked the assistance of a great military leader of mainland Greece, Pyrrhus, King of Epirus, who campaigned against both the Romans and the Carthaginians (280–275 BCE), but achieved only the costly and crippling victories to whose type he gave his name. He could not destroy the Roman threat to the western Greeks. Within a few years they were caught up willynilly in a struggle between Rome and Carthage in which the whole western Mediterranean was at stake – the Punic Wars.

THE PUNIC WARS

The Punic Wars form a duel of more than a century. Their name comes from the Roman rendering of the word Phoenician and, unfortunately, we have only the Roman version of what happened. There were three bursts of fighting, but the first two settled the question of preponderance. In the first (264–241 BCE),

This bone tablet, found in Palestrina and dating from the first half of the 3rd century BCE, shows a Roman soldier during the time of the republic.

the Romans began naval warfare on a large scale for the first time. With their new fleet they took Sicily and established themselves in Sardinia and Corsica. Syracuse abandoned an earlier alliance with Carthage, and western Sicily and Sardinia became the first Roman provinces, a momentous step, in 227 BCE.

This was only round one. As the end of the third century approached, the final outcome was still not discernible and there is still argument about which side, in this touchy situation, was responsible for the outbreak of the Second Punic War (218–201 BCE), the greatest of the three. It was fought in a greatly extended theatre, for when it began the Carthaginians were established in Spain. Some of the Greek cities there had been promised Roman protection. When one of them was attacked and sacked by a Carthaginian general, Hannibal, the war began. It is famous for Hannibal's great march to Italy and passage of the Alps with an army including elephants and for its culmination in the crushing Carthaginian victories of Lake Trasimene and Cannae (217 and 216 BCE), where a Roman army twice the size of Hannibal's was destroyed. At this point Rome's grasp on Italy was badly shaken; some of her allies and subordinates began to look at Carthaginian power with a new respect. Virtually all the south changed sides, though central Italy remained loyal. With no resources save her own exertions and the great advantage that Hannibal lacked the numbers needed to besiege Rome, Rome hung on and saved herself. Hannibal campaigned in an increasingly denuded countryside far

from his base. The Romans mercilessly destroyed Capua, a rebellious ally, without Hannibal coming to help her, and then boldly embarked upon a strategy of striking at Carthage in her own possessions, especially in Spain. In 209 BCE "New Carthage" (Cartagena) was taken by the Romans. When an attempt by Hannibal's younger brother to reinforce him was beaten off in 207 BCE the Romans transferred their offensives to Africa itself. There, at last, Hannibal had to follow them to meet his defeat at Zama in 202 BCE, the end of the war.

The defeat of Pyrrhus, King of Epirus, by the Romans in 275 BCE was a blow to the Greek world.

Carthage, a colony founded in the 9th century BCE by the Phoenicians of Tyre, was destroyed by the Roman general Scipio Aemilianus in 146 BCE, at the end of the Third Punic War. The surviving ruins, such as these, date from the new city that was founded by Julius Caesar in the Roman period. Recent excavations have revealed traces of the original Phoenician city and its port.

Roman gains in the Punic Wars

The outbreak of hostilities between Rome and
Carthage in 264 BCE was the beginning of a long
period of fighting known as the Punic Wars. The
battleground was enormous, extending as far as New
Carthage on the Iberian peninsula and throughout
Italy. During the wars, Rome also began incursions
into the eastern Mediterranean, which led to the
eventual conquest of the Greek territories. The conflict
ended in 146 BCE when the city of Carthage was totally
destroyed by the Romans. In just over one century,
they had unquestionably become the masters of the
Mediterranean, a situation reflected in their use of the
term *Mare nostrum* – "our sea".

*Publius Cornelius Scipio, depicted in this bust, was known
as "Africanus" because of his African campaigns during
the Second Punic War. He came from the aristocratic
Cornelius family, which was renowned for its military
achievements in the long struggle against Carthage.*

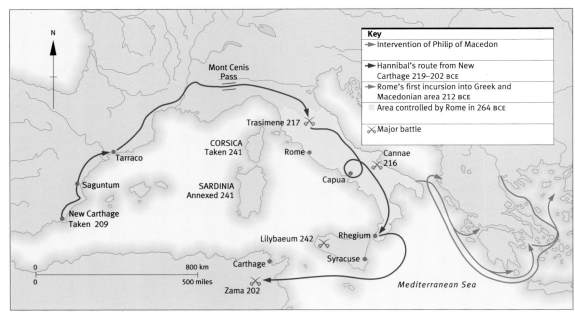

*The above map shows the area affected by the Punic Wars, as well as the dates
of all the major battles and of the Roman successes.*

A Roman warship is depicted on this bas-relief found at the site of the Oracle of Fortuna Primigenia in Praeneste, near Rome. The bas-relief is probably from a memorial dedicated to Mark Antony (c.83–30 BCE).

This battle settled more than a war; it decided the fate of the whole western Mediterranean. Once the Po valley was absorbed early in the second century BCE, Italy was, whatever the forms, henceforth a single state ruled from Rome. The peace imposed on Carthage was humiliating and crippling. Roman vengeance pursued Hannibal himself and drove him to exile at the Seleucid court. Because Syracuse had once more allied with Carthage during the war, her presumption was punished by the loss of her independence; she was the last Greek state in the island. The whole of Sicily was now Roman, as was southern Spain, where another province was set up.

ROME TURNS EAST

Roman expansion was not limited to the western Mediterranean. Events there opened the way to the East. At the end of the Second Punic War it is tempting to imagine Rome at a parting of the ways. On the one hand lay the alternative of moderation and the maintenance of security in the West, on the other that of expansion and imperialism in the East. Yet this over-simplifies reality. Eastern and Western issues were already too entangled to sustain so simple an antithesis. As early as 228 BCE the Romans had been admitted to the Greek Isthmian games; it was a recognition, even if only formal, that for some Greeks they were already a civilized power and part of the Hellenistic world. Through Macedon, that world had already been involved directly in the wars of Italy, for Macedon had allied with Carthage; Rome had therefore taken the side of Greek cities opposed to Macedon and thus begun to dabble in Greek politics. When a direct appeal for help against Macedon and the Seleucids came from Athens, Rhodes and a king of Pergamon in 200 BCE, the Romans were already psychologically ready to commit themselves to Eastern enterprise. It is unlikely,

though, that any of them saw that this could be the beginning of a series of adventures from which would emerge a Hellenistic world dominated by the republic.

Another change in Roman attitudes was not yet complete, but was beginning to be effective. When the struggle with Carthage

began, most upper-class Romans probably saw it as essentially defensive. Some went on fearing even the crippled enemy left after Zama. The call of Cato in the middle of the next century – "Carthage must be destroyed" – was to be famous as an expression of an implacable hostility arising from fear. None the less, the provinces won by war had begun to awake Romans' minds to other possibilities and soon supplied other motives for its continuation. Slaves and gold from Sardinia, Spain and Sicily were soon opening the eyes of Romans to what the rewards of empire might be. These countries were not treated like mainland Italy, as allies, but as resource pools to be administered and taxed. A tradition grew up under the republic, too, of generals distributing some of the spoils of victory to their troops.

THE GROWTH OF THE ROMAN EMPIRE

THE TWISTS AND TURNS are complicated, but the main stages of Roman expansion in the East in the second century BCE are obvious enough. The conquest and reduction of Macedon to a province was accomplished in a series of wars ending in 148 BCE; the phalanxes were not what they had been, nor Macedonian generalship. On the way the cities of Greece had also been reduced to vassalage and forced to send hostages to Rome. An intervention by a Syrian king led to the first passage of Roman forces to Asia Minor; next came the disappearance of the kingdom of Pergamon, Roman hegemony in the Aegean, and the establishment of the new province of Asia in 133 BCE. Elsewhere, the conquest of the remainder of Spain except the northwest, the organization of a tributary confederacy in Illyria, and the provincial organization of southern France in 121 BCE,

At the beginning of the 6th century BCE, the Greeks founded Emporiae on the northern Catalan coast. In the 3rd century BCE the city's port played a significant role in the Second Punic War. Emporiae later became part of the Roman Empire and enjoyed a period of great economic splendour, during which a new Roman city was built next to the original Greek one.

meant that the coasts from Gibraltar to Thessaly were all under Roman rule. Finally, the chance long sought by the enemies of Carthage came in 149 BCE with the start of the third and last Punic War. Three years later the city was destroyed, ploughs were run over its site and a new Roman province, Africa, existed in its stead.

The Roman expansion into southern France left a considerable mark on the architecture of the region. This commemorative arch in Saint-Rémy in Provence stands at what was once the entrance to the Roman city of Glanum.

This 1st-century BCE frieze was probably a monument to Gelio Publicola, who was censor in 70 BCE. The scene depicts the census being carried out in Rome. On the left, a citizen is being registered at a counter. The figures on the right are preparing to perform sacrifices.

THE IMPERIAL ADMINISTRATION

Thus was the empire made by the republic. Like all empires, but perhaps more obviously than any earlier one, its appearance owed as much to chance as to design. Fear, idealism and eventually cupidity were the mingled impulses which sent the legions further and further afield. Military power was the ultimate basis of the Roman Empire, and it was kept up by expansion. Numbers were decisive in overcoming Carthaginian experience and tenacity and the Roman army was large. It could draw upon an expanding pool of first-class manpower available from allies and satellites, and republican rule brought order and regular government to new subjects. The basic units of the empire were its provinces, each ruled by a governor with proconsular powers whose posting was formally for one year. Beside him stood a taxing officer.

Empire inevitably had political consequences at home. In the first place it made it even more difficult to ensure popular participation – that is, the participation of poor citizens – in government. Prolonged warfare reinforced the day-to-day power and the moral authority of the Senate, and it must be said that its record was a remarkable one. Yet the expansion of territory carried even further shortcomings already apparent in the extension of Roman rule over Italy. Serious and novel problems arose. One was posed by the new opportunities war and empire gave to generals and provincial governors. The fortunes to be made, and made quickly, were immense; not until the days of the Spanish *conquistadores* or the British East India Company were such prizes so easily available to

This beautiful silver dish dates from the 4th century CE. It is part of the Mildenhall Treasure – the household silver of a rich Roman family – found in a field in Suffolk, England, in 1942. The treasure, which was probably buried to save it from Saxon raiders, demonstrates the great wealth of some of the Romans who settled in the conquered territories.

those in the right place at the right time. Much of this was legal; some was simply looting and theft. Significantly, in 149 BCE a special court was created to deal with illegal extortion by officials. Whatever its nature, access to this wealth could only be obtained through participation in politics, for it was from the Senate that governors were chosen for the new provinces and it was the Senate which appointed the tax-gatherers who accompanied them from among the wealthy but non-noble class of *equites*, or knights.

CONSTITUTIONAL PROBLEMS

One constitutional weakness arose because the principle of annual election of magistrates had more and more frequently to be set aside in practice. War and rebellion in the provinces provided emergencies which consuls elected for their political skill might well find beyond them. Inevitably, proconsular power fell into the hands of those who could deal with emergencies effectively, usually proven generals. It is a mistake to think of the republic's commanders as professional soldiers in the modern sense; they were members of the ruling class who might expect in a successful career to be civil servants, judges, barristers, politicians and even priests. One key to the administrative proficiency of Rome was its acceptance of the principle of non-specialization in its rulers. None the less, a general who stayed years with his army became a different sort of political animal from the proconsuls of the early republic who commanded an army for one campaign and then returned to Rome and politics. Paradoxically, it was a weakness that the provincial governorships were themselves annual. In that lay a temptation to make hay while the sun shone. If this was one way by which irresponsibility crept into the administrative structure, there was a corresponding tendency for successful generals long in the field to draw to themselves the loyalty soldiers owed to the republic. Finally, there was even a kind of socialized corruption, for all Roman citizens benefited from an empire which made possible their exemption from any direct taxation; the provinces were to pay for the homeland. Awareness of such evils lay behind much moralizing condemnation and talk of decline which arose in the first century BCE, when their impact became fatal.

CONTINUING HELLENIZATION

Another change brought by empire was a further spread of Hellenization. Here there are difficulties of definition. In some measure,

The Romans loved Greek art, particularly statuary. This statue of Venus Genetrix is a Roman copy of a 5th-century BCE Greek statue attributed to the sculptor Callimachus.

Roman culture was already Hellenized before conquest went beyond Italy. The republic's conscious espousal of the cause of the Greek cities' independence of Macedon was a symptom. On the other hand, whatever Rome already possessed, there was much that could be hers only after more direct contact with the Hellenized world. In the last resort, Rome looked to many Greeks like another barbarian power, almost as bad as Carthage. There is symbolism in the legend of the death of Archimedes, struck down while pondering geometrical problems in the sand, by the sword of a Roman soldier who did not know who he was.

HELLENISTIC INFLUENCES

With empire contact with the Hellenized world became direct and the flow of Hellenistic influence manifold and frequent. Later ages were to wonder at the Roman passion for baths; the habit was one they had learnt from the Hellenized East. The first Roman literature was translated Greek drama and the first Latin comedies were imitations of Greek models. Art began to flow to Rome through pilfering and looting, but Greek style – above all its architecture – was already familiar from the western cities. There was a movement of people, too. One of the thousand hostages sent to Rome from the Greek cities in the middle of the second century BCE was Polybius, who provided Rome with its first scientific history in the tradition of Thucydides. His history of the years 220–146 BCE was a conscious exploration of a phenomenon which he felt to mark a new epoch, Rome's success in overthrowing Carthage and conquering the Hellenistic world. He first among historians recognized a complement to the earlier civilizing work of Alexander in the new unity given to the Mediterranean by Rome. He also admired the disinterested air Romans appeared to bring to imperial government – a reminder to be set against the Romans' own denunciation of their wickednesses under the late republic.

STABILITY

Rome's greatest triumph rested on the bringing of peace and it was a second great Hellenistic age in which travellers could move from one end to another of the Mediterranean without hindrance. The essential qualities of the structure which sustained it were already there under the republic, above all in the cosmopolitanism encouraged by Roman administration, which sought not to impose a uniform pattern of life but only to collect taxes, keep the peace and regulate the quarrels of men by a common law. The great achievements of Roman jurisprudence lay still far ahead, but the early republic in about 450 BCE launched Roman law on its history of definition by the consolidation of the Twelve Tables which little Roman boys lucky enough to go to school had still to get by heart hundreds of years later. On them was eventually built a framework within which many cultures might survive to contribute to a common civilization.

THE DECLINE OF THE REPUBLIC

IT IS CONVENIENT to finish the story of the spread of the rule of the republic to its limits before considering how such success in the end proved fatal. Transalpine Gaul (southern France) was a province in 121 BCE but (like north Italy) it remained troubled from time to time by the incursions of Celtic tribes. The Po

valley was given provincial status as Cisalpine Gaul in 89 BCE and nearly forty years later (51 BCE) the rest of Gaul – roughly northern France and Belgium – was conquered and with that the Celtic danger effectively came to an end. Meanwhile there had been further conquests in the East. The last king of Pergamon had bequeathed his kingdom to Rome in 133 BCE. There followed the acquisition of Cilicia in the early first century BCE, and then a series of wars with Mithridates, King of Pontus, a state on the Black Sea. The outcome was the reorganization of the Near East, Rome being left with possession of a coast running from Egypt to the Black Sea, all of which was divided between client kingdoms or provinces (one was named "Asia"). Finally, Cyprus was annexed in 58 BCE.

DOMESTIC CRISIS

Ironically, the counterpoint of continuing and apparently irresistible success abroad was

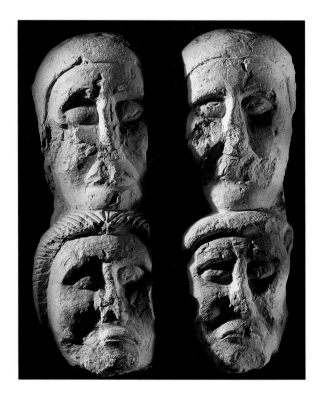

The heads of four dead Gallic warriors are depicted on a stone stele found in Provence, France. The piece is thought to date from the 3rd to 1st centuries BCE.

growing strife at home. The crux of the matter was the restriction of access to office to members of the ruling class. Electoral institutions and political conventions had come to work differently because of two grave long-term problems. The first was the gradual impoverishment of the Italian peasant who had been the typical figure of the early republic. It had several causes, but the root of the matter was the terrible cost of the Second Punic War. Not only had conscripted soldiers been absent for long years of almost continuous campaigns, but the physical damage to southern Italy was enormous. Meanwhile, those who were lucky enough to amass wealth in imperial enterprise laid it out

Hannibal, who used elephants in his army during the Second Punic War, was not the first enemy of Rome to do so. Indian elephants, such as the one depicted on this 3rd-century BCE Campanian dish, were first used in battle against the Romans by Pyrrhus, King of Epirus.

Marcus Tullius Cicero, born in 106 BCE, enjoyed a brilliant political career. He was a great orator who also composed philosophical and historical treatises. His prolific writing has given historians a valuable insight into the political and social issues of his time. Cicero was assassinated in 43 BCE.

in the only good investment available, land. The effect in the long run was to concentrate property in large estates usually worked by slaves made cheaper by the wars; there was no place on them for the smallholder, who now had to make his way to the city and fend for himself as best he could, a Roman citizen in name, but a proletarian in the making. Yet as a citizen he still had a vote. To those with wealth and political ambition he became someone to buy or to intimidate. Since the road to lucrative office lay through popular elections, the politics of the republic could hardly fail increasingly to reflect the power of money. This, too, had repercussions far and wide in Italy. Once votes had a price, the citizen proletariat of Rome was unlikely to welcome their continual devaluation by extending civic rights to other Italians, even though Rome's allies had to put up with conscription.

MILITARY SERVICE

Another problem was change in the army. The legions had more than four hundred years' history under the republic and their evolution can hardly be condensed in a simple formula, but if one is to be sought, it is perhaps best to say that the army became increasingly professional. After the Punic Wars it was impossible any longer to rely solely on soldiers fighting in such time as they could spare from farming. The burden of conscription had always been heavy and became unpopular. When campaigns carried men further and further afield for year after year, and

as garrisons had sometimes to remain for decades in conquered provinces, even the Roman pool of manpower showed signs of drying up. In 107 BCE a formal change registered what was happening: the property qualification for service was abolished. This was the work of a consul called Marius, who thus solved the problem of recruitment, for after this there were usually enough poor volunteers for conscription to be unnecessary. Military service still continued to be restricted to citizens, but there were many of these; in the end, though, service itself was to confer citizenship. Another innovation of Marius was to give the legions their "eagles", the standards so important to their *esprit de corps*, something between an idol and a modern regimental badge. Such changes gradually turned the army into a new kind of political force, available to a man like Marius who was an able general and much called upon for service in the provinces. He actually exacted a personal oath of allegiance from one army under his own command.

The widening gap of rich and poor in central Italy as peasant farming gave way to large estates bought (and stocked with slaves) with the spoils of empire, and the new possibilities open to political soldiers, proved fatal to the republic in the end. As the end of the second century BCE, the Gracchi brothers, Tribunes of the People, sought to do something about the social problem in the only way open to an agrarian economy, by land reform, reduction of senatorial power and a bigger role for the *equites* in government. They tried, in effect, to spread the wealth of empire, but their attempts only ended in their deaths. This itself marked the raising of the stakes in politics; in the last century of the republic factional bitterness reached its peak because politicians knew their lives might be forfeit. It also saw the beginning of what has been called the Roman revolution, for the

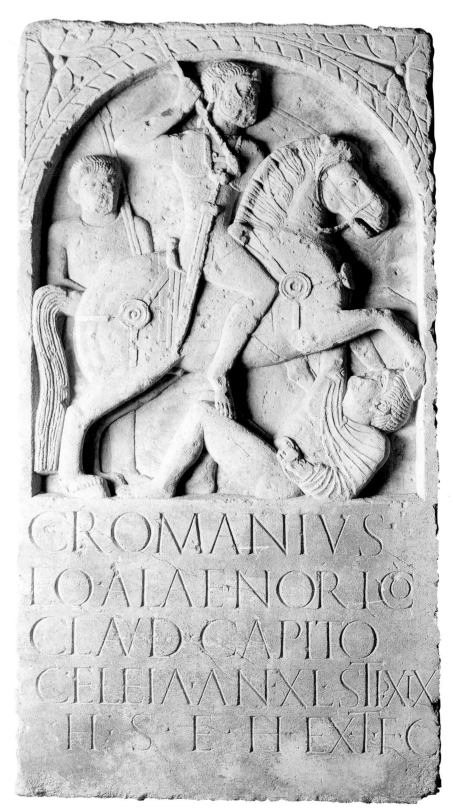

This funerary stele commemorates the death of a Roman soldier called Gaius Romanius Capitus. He was born in Slovenia in the 1st century CE and died at the age of 40.

Horse-drawn carriages were a common sight on the busy streets of Rome, as depicted on this Gallo-Roman bas-relief.

conventions of Roman politics were set aside when Tiberius Gracchus (the elder brother), then consul, persuaded the plebs to unseat the tribune who had vetoed his land-bill and thus announced that he would not accept the traditional circumvention of the popular will by the prerogative of a tribune to use his veto.

MARIUS SEIZES POWER

The final plunge of the republic into confusion was precipitated in 112 BCE by a new war when a north African king massacred a great number of Roman businessmen. Not long afterwards a wave of barbarian invaders in the north threatened Roman rule in Gaul. The emergency brought forward the consul Marius, who dealt successfully with the enemies of the republic, but at the cost of further constitutional innovation, for he was elected to the consulship for five years in succession.

He was, in fact, the first of a series of warlords who were to dominate the last century of the republic, for other wars rapidly followed. Demand grew for the extension of Roman citizenship to the other Latin and Italian states. In the end these allies (*socii*) revolted in what is somewhat misleadingly called the "Social War" in 90 BCE. They were only pacified with concessions which made nonsense of the notion that the Roman popular assemblies were the ultimate sovereign; citizenship was extended to most of Italy. Then came new Asian wars – from which emerged another general with political ambitions, Sulla. There was civil war, Marius died after once more being consul, and Sulla returned to Rome in 82 BCE to launch a dictatorship (voted by the Senate) with a ruthless "proscription" of his opponents (a posting of their names which signified that anyone who could do so was entitled to kill them), an assault on the popular powers of the

Plutarch describes Gaius Marius

"It was a hard war, but he [Gaius Marius] was not afraid of any undertaking, however great, and was not too proud to accept any task, however small. The advice he gave and his foresight into what was needed marked him out among the officers of his own rank, and he won the affection of the soldiers by showing that he could live as hard as they did and endure as much. Indeed it seems generally to be the case that our labours are eased when someone goes out of his way to share them with us; it has the effect of making the labour not seem forced. And what a Roman soldier likes most to see is his general eating his ration of bread with the rest, or sleeping on an ordinary bed, or joining in the work of digging a trench or a raising a palisade. The commanders whom they admire are not so much those who distribute honours and riches as those who take a share in their hardships and their dangers; they have more affection for those who are willing to join in their work than for those who indulge them in going easy.

"By these actions and in this way Marius won the hearts of the soldiers. First Libya and then Rome were soon full of his name and of his glory, and the men in the army wrote in their letters home that the African war could never be brought to a proper conclusion unless Marius were elected consul."

The republican general Gaius Marius.

An extract from "Gaius Marius", from *Fall of the Roman Republic: Six Lives* by Plutarch (c.46–c.120 CE), translated by Rex Warner.

constitution and an attempted restoration of those of the Senate.

POMPEY

One former supporter and protégé of Sulla was a young man whose name has passed into English as Pompey. Sulla had advanced his career by giving him posts normally held only by consuls and in 70 BCE he was elected to that office, too. He left for the East three years later to eliminate piracy from the Mediterranean and went on to conquer huge Asian territories in the wars against Pontus. Pompey's youth, success and outstanding ability began to

Mithridates VI (132–63 BCE), King of Pontus, tried to weaken the Roman presence in Asia Minor and the Aegean, taking advantage of the Greeks' hatred of the Romans. Defeated by Pompey, he committed suicide.

make him feared as a potential dictator. But the interplay of Roman politics was complicated. As the years passed, disorder increased in the capital and corruption in ruling circles. Fears of dictatorship were intensified, but the fears were those of one oligarchic faction among several and it was less and less clear where the danger lay. Moreover one danger went long disregarded before people awoke to it.

JULIUS CAESAR

IN 59 BCE another aristocrat, the nephew of Marius' wife, had been elected consul. This was the young Julius Caesar. For a time he had cooperated with Pompey. The consulship led him to the command of the

Lucius Cornelius Sulla (138–78 BCE) was a Roman general and statesman in the last era of the republic. From 82 to 79 BCE, he assumed the role of dictator, appointed by the Senate. He is remembered for his ruthless leadership style.

army of Gaul and a succession of brilliant campaigns in the next seven years ending in its complete conquest. Though he watched politics closely, these years kept Caesar away from Rome where gangsterism, corruption and murder disfigured public life and discredited the Senate. After them he was enormously rich and had a loyal, superbly experienced and confident army looking to him for the leadership which would give them pay, promotion and victory in the future. He was also a cool, patient and ruthless man. There is a story of him joking and playing at dice with some pirates who captured him. One of his jokes was that he would crucify them when he was freed. The pirates laughed, but crucify them he did.

Some senators suddenly became alarmed when this formidable man wished to remain in Gaul in command of his army and the province, although its conquest was complete, retaining command until the consular election. His opponents strove to get him recalled to face charges about illegalities during his consulship. Caesar then took the step which, though neither he nor anyone else knew it, was the beginning of the end of the republic. He led his army across the Rubicon, the boundary of his province, beginning a march which brought him in the end to Rome. This was in January 49 BCE. It was an act of treason, though he claimed to be defending the republic against its enemies.

Julius Caesar in Gaul

"On learning of his [Caesar's] arrival and the Roman preparations, the Veneti and the other tribes ... began to make ready for war on a scale commensurate with the seriousness of their peril. ... Their hopes of success were increased by the confidence they placed in the natural strength of their country. They knew that the roads were intersected by tidal inlets, and that sailing would be difficult for us on account of our ignorance of the waterways and the scarcity of harbours. ... And even if all their expectations were disappointed, they had a strong fleet, while we had no ships available and were unacquainted with the shoals, harbours, and islands of the coast on which we should have to fight. ... Having resolved to fight,

Gaius Julius Caesar (100–44 BCE) came from a well-known aristocratic family and was the main protagonist in the collapse of the Roman Republic. He also had a gift for self-promotion, which is demonstrated in his historical writing.

they fortified their strongholds, stocked them with corn from the fields, and assembled as many ships as possible on the coast of Venetia, where it was ... thought that Caesar would open hostilities. They secured the alliance of various tribes in the neighbourhood ... and summoned reinforcements from Britain, which faces that part of Gaul.

"In spite of the difficulties, Caesar had several strong reasons for undertaking this campaign: the unlawful detention of Roman knights, the revolt and renewal of hostilities by enemies who had submitted and given hostages, the large number of tribes leagued against him, and above all the danger that if these were left unpunished others might think themselves entitled to follow their example. Knowing, too, that nearly all the Gauls were fond of political change and quickly and easily provoked to war, and that all men naturally love freedom and hate servitude, he thought it advisable to divide his forces and distribute them over a wider area before more tribes could join the coalition."

An extract from Book III of *The Conquest of Gaul* by Julius Caesar, translated by S. A. Handford.

The Roman army

The emperor Marcus Aurelius celebrates his victories over the barbarians in the Danube region with a triumphal march. Growing pressure from the Germanic peoples posed a serious threat to the empire's northern frontier at the end of the 2nd century BCE. This meant that most imperial soldiers were stationed in camps near the empire's borders, where distance from the cities and from their families tended to encourage cohesion among the troops.

In the time of the republic, there was little difference between civil and military powers. However, after the Punic Wars, it was clearly not viable for the army to continue to depend on soldiers who had to tend their land for part of each year. From the end of the 2nd century BCE, army recruits were no longer required to be landowners. This made it possible to abolish conscription – there were enough eager, poor volunteers to form a professional army. Later, non-Roman citizens were allowed to join the army, and military service became a means of earning citizenship. These reforms greatly increased the power of the army's generals, who depended on their troops' loyalty.

During the imperial era, the army was divided into three separate bodies: the imperial guard, known as the praetorians (9,000 élite soldiers, with their headquarters in Rome); the 30 legions (180,000 soldiers who were Roman citizens); and the auxiliary troops (200,000 soldiers who could apply for citizenship at the end of their service).

CAESAR TAKES POWER

In its extremity the Senate called Pompey to defend the republic. Without forces in Italy, Pompey withdrew across the Adriatic to raise an army. The consuls and most of the Senate went with him. Civil war was now inevitable. Caesar marched quickly to Spain to defeat seven legions there which were loyal to Pompey; they were then mildly treated in order to win over as many of the soldiers as possible. Ruthless and even cruel though he could be, mildness to his political opponents was politic and prudent; he did not propose to imitate Sulla, said Caesar. Then he went after Pompey, chasing him to Egypt, where he was murdered. Caesar stayed long enough to dabble in an Egyptian civil war and became, almost incidentally, the lover of the legendary Cleopatra. Then he went back to Rome, to embark almost at once for Africa and defeat a Roman army there which opposed him. Finally, he returned again to Spain and destroyed a force raised by Pompey's sons. This was in 45 BCE, four years after the crossing of the Rubicon.

Brilliance like this was not just a matter of winning battles. Brief though Caesar's recent visits to Rome had been, he had organized his political support carefully and packed the Senate with his men. The victories brought him great honours and real power. He was voted dictator for life and became in effect a monarch in all but name. His power he used without much regard for the susceptibilities of politicians and without showing an imaginativeness which suggests his rule would have been successful in the long term,

The town of Orange (Arausio), in southern France, was originally founded as a colony for Roman military veterans by Julius Caesar. This triumphal arch, which is decorated with battle scenes, was erected in Caesar's honour to commemorate the event.

The expansion of the Roman Empire

By the end of the 1st century BCE, the Roman Empire extended throughout most Mediterranean countries in the south and reached as far as the Rhine in the north. In order to make such impressive expansion possible, it had been necessary to eliminate Carthage, Rome's greatest opponent in the western Mediterranean, and to push further into the lands of the ancient Hellenistic kingdoms. The conquest of these new territories greatly enriched Rome, both materially and culturally. The burgeoning empire's immense size also challenged the capacities of her military and political organizations, which were obliged to adapt quickly to the new situation.

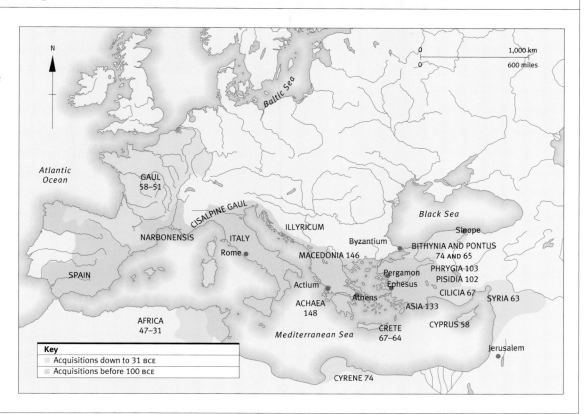

Key
Acquisitions down to 31 BCE
Acquisitions before 100 BCE

though he imposed order in the Roman streets, and undertook steps to end the power of the money-lenders in politics. To one reform in particular the future of Europe was to owe much – the introduction of the Julian calendar. Like much else we think of as Roman, it came from Hellenistic Alexandria, where an astronomer suggested to Caesar that the year of 365 days, with an extra day each fourth year, would make it possible to emerge from the complexities of the traditional Roman calendar. The new calendar began on 1 January 45 BCE.

THE END OF THE REPUBLIC

Fifteen months after the beginning of the new calendar, Caesar was dead, struck down in the Senate on 15 March 44 BCE at the height of his success. His assassins' motives were complex. The timing was undoubtedly affected by the knowledge that he planned a great Eastern campaign against the Parthians. Were he to join his army, it might be to return again in triumph, more unassailable than ever. There had been talk of a kingship; a Hellenistic despotism was envisaged by some. The complicated motives of his enemies were given respectability by the distaste some felt for the flagrant affront to republican tradition in the *de facto* despotism of one man. Minor acts of disrespect for the constitution antagonized others and in the end his assassins were a mixed bag of disappointed soldiers, interested oligarchs and offended conservatives.

His murderers had no answer to the problems which Caesar had not had the time and their predecessors had so conspicuously failed

As well as reorganizing the ancient Forum, Julius Caesar built a new one next to it. The original Forum had become rather small for a city now at the head of a vast empire. Before construction work could begin, Caesar had to expropriate an area of private houses, at great expense. His new Forum was rectangular in shape and was surrounded by porticos lined with shops, the ruins of which can be seen here behind the double colonnade.

to solve. Nor could they protect themselves for long. The republic was pronounced restored, but Caesar's acts were confirmed. There was a revulsion of feeling against the conspirators, who soon had to flee the city. Within two years they were dead and Julius Caesar was proclaimed a god. The republic was moribund, too. Damaged fatally long before the crossing of the Rubicon, the heart had gone out of its constitution whatever attempts were made to restore it. Yet its myths, its ideology and forms lived on in a romanized Italy. Romans could not bring themselves to turn their backs on the institutional heritage and admit that they had done with it. When eventually they did, they had already ceased in all but name to resemble the Romans of the republic.

This statue represents Julius Caesar, the great general and statesman who defeated his rival Pompey to become the ruler of Rome. Caesar is famous for conquering Gaul and for his remarkable literary accounts of his military campaigns. All the subsequent Roman emperors took the official title of Caesar, perhaps in the hope that their predecessor's glory would be reflected on them.

2 *THE ROMAN ACHIEVEMENT*

IF THE GREEK CONTRIBUTION to civilization was essentially mental and spiritual, that of Rome was structural and practical; its essence was the empire itself. Though no man is an empire, not even the great Alexander, its nature and government were to an astonishing degree the creation of one man of outstanding ability, Julius Caesar's great-nephew and adopted heir, Octavian.

THE AUGUSTAN AGE

LATER OCTAVIAN WAS to be known as Caesar Augustus. An age has been named after him; his name gave an adjective to posterity. Sometimes one has the feeling that Octavian invented almost everything that characterized imperial Rome, from the new Praetorian Guard, which was the first military force stationed permanently in the capital, to the taxation of bachelors. One reason for this impression (though only one) is that he was a master of

Minted in 32 BCE, this coin bears Mark Antony's portrait (top). The Armenian tiara in the background symbolizes his military conquests in the East. On the reverse side (bottom) is a portrait of Cleopatra, the Egyptian queen with whom Mark Antony allied himself.

public relations; significantly, more representations of him than of any other Roman emperor have come down to us.

Though a Caesar, Octavian came of a junior branch. From Julius (whom he succeeded at the age of eighteen) he inherited aristocratic connexions, great wealth and military support. For a time he cooperated with one of Caesar's henchmen, Mark Antony, in a ferocious series of proscriptions to destroy the party which had murdered the great dictator. Mark Antony's departure to win victories in the East, failure to do so and injudicious marriage to Cleopatra, Julius Caesar's sometime mistress, gave Octavian further opportunities. He fought in the name of the republic against a threat that Antony might make a proconsular return bringing oriental monarchy in his baggage-train. The victory of Actium (31 BCE) was followed by the legendary suicides of Antony and Cleopatra; the kingdom of the Ptolemies came to an end and Egypt too was annexed as a province of Rome.

Time chart (32 BCE–193 CE)

		14–68 CE	69–96 CE	117 CE
	27 BCE–14 CE Reign of Octavian (Augustus)	Julio-Claudian Dynasty: Tiberius, Caligula, Claudius and Nero	Flavian Dynasty: Vespasian, Titus and Domitian	Empire reaches its maximum extent with Trajan's conquests

50 BCE	25 BCE	0	50 CE	100 CE	150 CE	200 CE

| | 32–31 BCE Octavian's war against Antony and Cleopatra | | 68–69 CE Year of the Four Emperors | 96–192 CE Adoptive emperors: Nerva, Trajan, Hadrian, Antoninus Pius, Marcus Aurelius and Commodus | | 193 CE Septimius Severus founds Severan Dynasty |

The Gemma Augustae is a cameo from c.10 CE in which Augustus is shown, enthroned as Jupiter, beside the goddess Roma. In front of the emperor, Germanicus is preparing for his next expedition, while Tiberius alights from a chariot driven by Victoria. In the lower section, Roman soldiers are raising a monument to Victoria and auxiliaries are leading their barbarian captives away.

AUGUSTUS AS CONSUL

The annexation of Egypt signalled the end of civil war. Octavian returned to become consul. He had every card in his hand and judiciously refrained from playing them, leaving it to his opponents to recognize his strength. In 27 BCE he carried out what he called a republican restoration with the support of a Senate whose republican membership, purged and weakened by civil war and proscription, he reconciled to his real primacy by his careful preservation of forms. He re-established the reality of his great-uncle's power behind a facade of republican piety. He was *imperator* only by virtue of his command of the troops of the frontier provinces – but that was where the bulk of the legions were. As old soldiers of his and his great-uncle's armies returned to retirement, they were duly settled on smallholdings and were appropriately grateful. His consulship was prolonged from year to year and in 27 BCE he was given the honorific title of Augustus, the name by which he is remembered. At Rome, though, he was formally and usually called by his family name, or was identified as *princeps*, first citizen. As the years passed Augustus' power still grew. The Senate accorded him a right of interference in those provinces which it formally ruled (that is, those where there was no need to keep a garrison army). He was voted the tribunician power. His special status was enhanced and formalized by a new recognition of his state or *dignitas*, as the Romans called it; he sat between the two consuls after his resignation from that office in 23 BCE and his business was given precedence in the agenda of the Senate. Finally, in 12 BCE he became *pontifex maximus*, the head of the official cult, as his great-uncle had been. The forms of the republic with their popular elections and senatorial elections were maintained, but Augustus said who should be elected.

THE BENEVOLENT DESPOT

The political reality masked by the ascendancy enjoyed by Augustus was the rise to domination within the ruling class of men who owed their position to the Caesars. But the new élites were not to be allowed to behave like the old. The Augustan benevolent despotism regularized the provincial administration and army by putting them into obedient and

This marble statue of Augustus is a copy of a bronze piece that was made around 20 BCE. The emperor is portrayed as both a triumphant general and a god – his bare feet symbolize his divinity. At his side is Cupid on a dolphin, respresenting Augustus' descent from Venus.

The Ara Pacis Augustae is a monument dedicated to the peace established by the emperor Augustus. This fragment from the frieze shows a procession that includes members of the royal family. Augustus' son-in-law Agrippa is seen walking behind the servants. Behind Agrippa are his young son Gaius Caesar and his wife Julia (the daughter of Augustus).

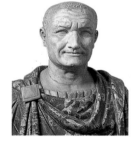

Vespasian (9–81 CE) enjoyed a brilliant military career. On the death of the emperor Vitellius in 69, during the civil war, the Eastern legions proclaimed Vespasian emperor. He reestablished order in the empire and secured its borders by creating permanent military encampments on the Danube and the Rhine.

salaried hands. The conscious resuscitation of republican tradition and festivals had a part to play in this, too. Augustan government was heavily tinged with concern for moral revival; the virtues of ancient Rome seemed to some to live again. Ovid, a poet of pleasure and love, was packed off to exile in the Black Sea when a sexual scandal at the edge of the imperial family provided an excuse. When to this official austerity is added the peace which marked most of the reign and the great visible monuments of the Roman architects and engineers, the reputation of the Augustan age is hardly surprising. After his death in 14 CE Augustus was deified, as Julius Caesar had been.

MONARCHY AND CIVIL WAR

Augustus intended to be succeeded by a member of his own family. Although he respected republican forms (and they were to endure with remarkable tenacity) Rome was now really a monarchy and this was demonstrated by the succession of five members of the same family. Augustus' only child was a daughter; his immediate successor was his adopted stepson, Tiberius, one of his daughter's three husbands. The last of his descendants to reign, Nero, died in 68 CE.

The rulers of the classical world did not usually live easy lives. Some Roman emperors had great mirrors installed at the corners of the corridors of their palaces so that would-be assassins could not lurk around them. Tiberius himself may have not have died a natural death, and none of his four successors did. The fact is significant of the weaknesses inherent in Augustus' legacy. There was still scope for pinpricks from a Senate which formally continued to appoint the first magistrate, and always room for intrigue and cabal about the court and imperial household. Yet the Senate could never hope to recover authority, for the ultimate basis of power was always military. If there was confusion and indecision at the centre, then the soldiers would decide. This was what happened in the first great burst of civil war to shake the empire, in the year of the Four Emperors, 69 CE, from which there emerged Vespasian, the grandson of a centurion and far from an aristocrat. The first magistracy had passed out of the hands of the great Roman families.

THE ANTONINES

When Vespasian's younger son was murdered in 96 CE this upstart house came to an end. Its successor was an elderly senator, Nerva. He solved the problem of succession by breaking with attempts to ensure natural dynastic continuity. Instead, he institutionalized the practice of adoption to which Augustus had been driven. The result was a succession of four emperors, Trajan, Hadrian, Antoninus Pius and Marcus Aurelius, who gave the empire a century of good government; it has been named (after the third of them) the age of the Antonines. All of them came of families with provincial roots; they were evidence of the degree to which the empire was a cosmopolitan reality, the framework of the post-Hellenistic world of the West, and not merely the property of the Italian-born. Adoption made it easier to find candidates upon whom army, provinces and Senate could agree, but this golden age came to an end with a reversion to the hereditary principle, the succession of Commodus, son of Marcus Aurelius. He was murdered in 192 CE, and a new 69 CE followed when, in the following year, there were again four emperors, each acclaimed by his own army. The Illyrian army prevailed in the end, imposing an African general. Other and later emperors were to be the nominees of soldiers too; bad times lay ahead.

THE LIMITS OF EMPIRE

The emperors now ruled a far larger area than had Augustus. In the north Julius

This is the only bronze equestrian statue known to have survived from the classical era. It depicts the emperor Marcus Aurelius (161–180 CE), who prided himself on his love of culture. His own writings include the *Soliloquies*, which strongly reflect his Stoic philosophy.

Augustus and the Roman Empire

"Augustus kept for himself all the more vigorous provinces – those that could not be safely administered by an annual governor; the remainder went to proconsuls chosen by lot. Yet, as occasion arose, he would change the status of provinces from imperial to senatorial, or contrariwise, and paid frequent visits to either sort. Finding that certain city-states which had treaties of alliance with Rome were ruining themselves through political irresponsibility, he took away their independence; but also granted subsidies to others crippled by public debts, rebuilt some cities which had been devastated by earthquakes, and even awarded Latin rights or full citizenship to states that could show a record of faithful service in the Roman cause. So ... Augustus inspected every province of the Empire, except Sardinia and North Africa. ... He nearly always restored the kingdoms which he had conquered to their defeated dynasties, or combined them with others, and followed a policy of linking together his royal allies by mutual ties of friendship or intermarriage, which he was never slow to propose. Nor did he treat them otherwise than as integral parts of the Empire, showing them all consideration and finding guardians for those who were not yet old enough to rule, until they came of age. ... He also brought up many of their children with his own, and gave them the same education."

An extract from "Augustus", v. 47–8, from
The Twelve Caesars by Suetonius (c.69–c.150 CE),
translated by Robert Graves.

Caesar had carried out reconnaissances into Britain and Germany, but had left Gaul with the Channel and the Rhine as its frontiers. Augustus pressed into Germany, and also up to the Danube from the south. The Danube eventually became the frontier of the empire, but incursions beyond the Rhine were less successful and the frontier was not stabilized on the Elbe as Augustus had hoped. Instead, a grave shock had been given to Roman confidence in 9 CE when the Teutonic tribes led by Arminius (in whom later Germans were to see a national hero) destroyed three legions. The ground was never recovered, nor the legions, for their numbers were thought so ill-omened that they never again appear in the army lists. Eight remained stationed along the Rhine, the most strongly held part of the frontier because of the dangers which lay beyond it.

Elsewhere, Roman rule still advanced. In 43 CE Claudius began the conquest of Britain, which was carried to its furthest enduring limit when Hadrian's Wall was built across the north as an effective boundary eighty or so years later. In 42 CE Mauretania had become a province. In the East Trajan conquered Dacia, the later Romania, in 105 CE, but this was more than a century and a half after a quarrel which was to be long-lasting had opened in Asia.

ROME AND PARTHIA

Rome had first faced Parthia on the Euphrates when Sulla's army campaigned there in 92 BCE. Nothing of importance followed until thirty years later when Roman armies began to advance against Armenia. Two spheres of influence overlapped there and Pompey at one moment arbitrated between the Armenian and Parthian kings in a boundary dispute. Then, in 54 BCE, the Roman politician Crassus launched an invasion of Parthia across the Euphrates. Within a few weeks he was dead and a Roman army of forty thousand destroyed. It was one of the worst military disasters of Roman history. Evidently there was a new great power in Asia. The Parthian army had more than good mounted archers to it by this time. It also had heavy cavalry of unrivalled quality, the cataphracts, mail-clad horsemen with their mounts mailed, too, charging home with a heavy lance. The fame of their great horses even awoke the envy of the distant Chinese.

Hadrian's Wall was built to defend the empire's northern frontier in Britain during the reign of Hadrian (117–138 CE). The wall was 75 miles (120 km) long and relied on 17 heavily guarded fortresses, at which infantry units were garrisoned. Between the fortresses, smaller "milecastles" were built, and between each of these stood two lookout towers, allowing close observation of the surrounding terrain.

After this, the eastern frontier on the Euphrates was to remain undisturbed for a century, but the Parthians did not endear themselves to Rome. They dabbled in the politics of the civil war, harassing Syria and encouraging unrest among the Palestinian Jews. Mark Antony had to retreat in disgrace and distress to Armenia after losing thirty-five thousand men in a disastrous campaign against them. But Parthia suffered from internal divisions, too, and in 20 BCE Augustus was able to obtain the return of the Roman standards taken from Crassus and thankfully set aside any need to attack Parthia for reasons of honour. Yet the likelihood of conflict persisted, both because of the sensitivity with which each power regarded Armenia and because of the instability of Parthia's dynastic politics. One emperor, Trajan, conquered the Parthian capital of Ctesiphon and fought his way down to the Persian Gulf, but his successor Hadrian wisely conciliated the Parthians by handing back much of his conquest.

THE *PAX ROMANA*

It was the Roman boast that their new subjects all benefited from the extension to them of the *Pax Romana*, the imperial peace which removed the threats of barbarian incursion or international strife. The claim has to be qualified by recognition of the violence with which many subject peoples resisted Roman rule, and the bloodshed this cost, but there is something in it. Within the frontiers there was order and peace as never before. In some places this permanently changed the patterns of settlement as new cities were founded in the East or descendants of Caesar's soldiers

Marcus Licinius Crassus (115–53 BCE) was one of the richest men in Rome in his day. A member of the first Triumvirate with Caesar and Pompey, Crassus was responsible for Asia Minor and Syria. In 53 BCE, in one of the greatest military disasters in Roman history, he was defeated by the Parthian army.

These detailed bas-reliefs decorate Trajan's Column, constructed in his Forum in Rome. The column commemorates the Romans' victory over the Dacians, which led to the annexation of Dacia (now Romania) to the empire at the beginning of the 2nd century CE. Various events from the campaign are depicted in the above scenes, including the emperor delivering speeches to his troops, the building of fortifications, and battles.

The imperial residences on the Palatine Hill

At the end of the 1st century CE, the emperor Domitian ordered that a large residential complex be built next to Tiberius' palace, extending throughout the central part of the Palatine Hill. The Domus Flavia was comprised of official buildings, each one huge: the throne room, the advisory chamber or *basilica*, the dining room and the libraries. It also had a large patio surrounded by marble columns. The Domus Augustia – a luxurious villa with several patios – was the emperor's private residence. To this, Domitian later added a stadium and thermal baths. The Domus Severiana, built in the time of Septimius Severus, in the late 2nd century CE, stands partly on a large platform jutting out from the hillside.

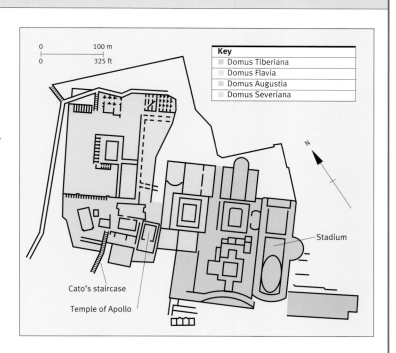

Key
- Domus Tiberiana
- Domus Flavia
- Domus Augustia
- Domus Severiana

0 100 m
0 325 ft

Stadium

Cato's staircase

Temple of Apollo

The Domus Tiberiana was built during the reign of Tiberius in the 1st century CE, above the Roman Forum. It was the first of the imperial buildings on the Palatine Hill, hence the word palatium (palace). In the 16th century CE, the Farnesian Orchards were established over this area, obscuring a large part of the remains.

The Porta Nigra in the Roman city of Treveri (now Trier, or Trèves) dates from the end of the 2nd century CE. The city became a major centre, as its favourable geographical situation allowed easy access to the military encampments along the Rhine. Treveri was the headquarters of the procurator of Belgium and the Two Germanias and, from the end of the 3rd century, it was one of the most important cities in the Western Empire.

were settled in new military colonies in Gaul. Sometimes there were even more far-reaching results. The adoption of the Rhine frontier permanently affected the history of Europe by its division of the Germanic peoples. Meanwhile, everywhere, as things settled down, a gradual romanization of the local notables occurred. They were encouraged to share a common civilization whose spread was made easier by the new swiftness of communication along the roads whose main purpose was the movement of the legions. Napoleon could not move couriers faster from Paris to Rome than could the emperors of the first century CE.

IMPERIAL ORGANIZATION

The empire was a huge area and required the solution of problems of government which had not been faced by Greeks or solved by Persians. A complex bureaucracy appeared, with remarkable scope. To cite one small example, the records of all officers of centurion rank and above (company commanders upwards, as it were) were centralized at Rome. The corps of provincial civil servants was the administrative armature, sustained by a practical reliance for many places upon the army, which did much more than merely fight. Bureaucracy was controlled by the adoption of fairly limited aims. These were above all fiscal; if the taxes came in, then Roman rule did not want to interfere in other ways with the operation of local custom. Rome was tolerant. It would provide the setting within which the example of its civilization would wean barbarians from their native ways. The reform of the administrators had begun under Augustus. The Senate still appointed to many posts on an annual basis, but the emperor's *legati* who acted for him in the frontier provinces held office at his pleasure. All the evidence is that, whatever the means were by which it was achieved, the administration underwent a notable improvement under the empire by comparison with the corruption of the last century of the republic. It was much more centralized and integrated than the satrapy system of Persia.

The cooperation of the subject peoples was tempted with a bait. First the republic and then the empire had been extended by granting citizenship to wider and wider numbers of Rome's subjects. It was an important privilege; among other things, as the Acts of the Apostles remind us, it carried with it rights of appeal from local courts to the emperor at Rome. On the granting of citizenship could be based the winning of the loyalties of local notables; more and more non-Romans make their appearance in the Senate and at Rome as the centuries pass. Finally, in 212 CE citizenship was granted to all free subjects of the empire.

COSMOPOLITANISM

The enlargement of the citizen class was an outstanding instance of Roman digestive power. The empire and the civilization it carried were unashamedly cosmopolitan. The administrative framework contained an astonishing variety of contrasts and diversities. They were held together not by an impartial despotism exercised by a Roman élite or a professional bureaucracy, but by a constitutional system which took local élites and romanized them. From the first century CE the senators themselves included only a dwindling number of men of Italian descent. Roman tolerance in this was diffused among other peoples. The empire was never a racial unity whose hierarchies were closed to non-Italians. Only one of its peoples, the Jews, felt strongly about the retention of their

In 312 BCE, the censor Appius Claudius gave orders for the Appian Way (below) to be paved, making it the first paved road in Rome. A vast network of similar roads was eventually constructed, enabling the empire's capital city to be connected to even its most remote provinces.

distinction within it, and that distinction rested on religion.

ROME'S GREEK HERITAGE

Already Hellenistic civilization had achieved a remarkable mixing of East and West; now Rome continued the process over an even wider area. The element in the new cosmopolitanism which was most obvious was, indeed, the Greek, for the Romans themselves made much of their inheritance from the Greeks, though it was the Greeks of the Hellenistic era with whom they were most at home. All educated Romans were bilingual and this illustrates the tradition upon which they drew. Latin was the official language and always remained the language of the army; it was spoken widely in the West and to judge by the military records, literacy in it was high. Greek was the *lingua franca* in the Eastern provinces, understood by all officials and merchants, and used in the courts if the litigants wished. Educated Romans grew up to read the Greek classics and drew from them their standards; the creation of a literature which could stand on an equal footing with the older was the laudable ambition of most Roman writers. In the first century CE they got nearest to this and the coincidence of a cultural and an imperial achievement is striking in Virgil, the conscious renewer of the epic tradition who was also the poet of imperial mission.

It may be that in this lies one clue to explain the peculiar feel of Roman culture. Perhaps it is the obviousness and pervasiveness of the Greek background which does much to deprive it of the air of novelty. Its weight was accentuated by the static, conservative concern of Roman thinkers. Between them, their attention was absorbed almost exclusively by the two foci provided by the

The Roman Empire owed its cosmopolitanism to its great size. This detail from a 3rd-century CE mosaic floor comes from a villa in the port of Hadrumetum (now Sousse) in the Roman province of Africa Proconsularis. Though the animals depicted are clearly inspired by African wildlife, the scene is quintessentially Roman, showing the triumphal procession of Dionysus, lord of the beasts and god of wine and ecstasy.

Latin language and literature

Latin, the official language throughout the empire, constitutes one of Roman civilization's greatest legacies. Evidence suggests that written Latin was in use as early as the 4th century BCE. Literary Latin, the earliest evidence of which dates from the 3rd century BCE, was to remain relatively unchanged for centuries. During the Middle Ages and the Renaissance, the principal philosophical or scientific works continued to be written in Latin, which had become an international cultural language. However, spoken Latin evolved much more quickly and became the basis of the various Romance languages.

Countless authors have been inspired by Roman literature over the centuries and its profound influence on later European literature is undeniable. The Romans cultivated literary genres that had already been established by the Greeks – drama, poetry and historic narrative. They also developed new genres, including satire, and placed great importance on the art of rhetoric.

This 4th-century mosaic, found in a house in northern Africa, is a testament to the veneration that the Romans felt for the poet Virgil, who lived in the 1st century BCE. Virgil is shown flanked by Calliope, Muse of Epic Poetry, and Melpomene, Muse of Tragedy. In his lap is a scroll of the Aeneid *displaying Book 8, in which the poet invokes the Muses.*

Greek inheritance and the moral and political traditions of the republic. Both lived on curiously and somewhat artificially in a material setting which more and more ceased to fit them. Formal education changed little in practice and content from century to century, for example. Livy, the great Roman historian, sought again to quicken republican virtues in his history, but not to criticize and reinterpret them. Even when Roman civilization was irreversibly urban the (almost extinct) virtues of the independent peasant continued to be celebrated and rich Romans longed (they said) to get away from it all to the simple life of the countryside. Roman sculpture only provided again what Greeks had already done better. The philosophies of Rome were Greek, too. Epicureanism and Stoicism held the centre of the stage; neo-Platonism was innovatory, but came from the East, as did the mystery religions which were eventually to provide Roman men and women with something their culture could not give them.

LAW, ENGINEERING AND TOWN PLANNING

The Romans were only great innovators in two practical fields, law and engineering. The achievements of the lawyers were relatively late; it was in the second and early third centuries CE that the jurisconsults began the

Discovered in the villa in Boscoreale, this fresco dates from 10 BCE and is an example of the pastoral style of painting that became highly popular in Rome from the time of Augustus. Nature was idealized and the virtues and simplicity of rural life were glorified while being portrayed in decidedly urban surroundings.

accumulation of commentary which would be so valuable a legacy to the future when codification passed their work to medieval Europe. In engineering – and Romans did not distinguish it from architecture – the quality of their achievement is more immediately impressive. It was a source of pride to the Romans and one of the few things in which they were sure they outstripped the Greeks. It was based on cheap labour: at Rome it was slaves and in the provinces often the unemployed legions on garrison duty in peaceful times who carried out the great works of

A tutor is depicted giving instruction to children from a rich family in this scene from a Roman tomb. Teaching methods in Rome were reformed during the 1st and 2nd centuries CE and education was divided into three grades: primary school, grammar school and rhetoric school.

Engineering and architecture

The Romans' engineering skills were outstanding. Great Roman monuments are surprising not only for their grandeur but also for the strength of their walls and vaults – a tribute to the expert construction techniques of their builders.

Until the 3rd century BCE, Roman buildings were made of wood and clay-brick and only city walls were built with superimposed blocks of cut stone. The use of cement, from the 3rd century BCE, revolutionized building methods. When a cement facade was not decorated with stone bas-reliefs or tiles the surface was usually covered with stucco and whitewashed.

From the 1st century BCE, the Romans used baked tiles, which, because of their refractory properties, were ideal for the construction of thermal baths.

The Greek tradition of huge columns and cut stone was upheld in the decoration of large public buildings. For the first time, interior areas were treated as more than just rooms to decorate: space and lighting were taken into account. Civil engineering projects, however, such as bridges and aqueducts, were designed to meet technical and functional rather than decorative needs.

This marble funerary bas-relief dates from the year 100 CE and, in memory of one of the building contractors for the project, represents the construction of a temple. The crane on the left was powered by slaves inside the enormous tread-wheel.

The road bridge across the Tagus River at Alcántara in Spain dates from the 1st century CE and is an example of the Roman administration's efforts to provide the provinces with an efficient communication system. The architect left an inscription, proudly declaring that the bridge "will last for always throughout time".

Work on the Pantheon in Rome was begun by Agrippa, Augustus' son-in-law, in 27 BCE. Agrippa's temple was later destroyed by fire and then rebuilt by Hadrian c.118–128 CE. Brick and six different types of concrete were used in the construction of the Pantheon, as well as coloured marble from many parts of the empire. Although the exterior of the structure is unremarkable, the interior is a large, impressive circular space surmounted by a huge hemispherical dome. A central hole, or oculus (eye), is the sole internal source of light. Seven niches, which originally contained statues of the planetary gods, ring the vestibule; as the sun moved round each was illuminated in turn by the ray of light from the roof, representing the sky god Jupiter. The Pantheon was a triumph of Roman engineering, as well as an important symbolic and religious building; the dome itself, made of concrete, weighs 5,000 tons and is carried on walls that are nearly 20 ft (6 m) thick.

Roman law

The first attempt to collate the laws that were in use in Rome took place c.450 BCE, when the *Twelve Tables* were inscribed and erected in the Roman Forum. As Roman law evolved, it covered mainly personal issues, such as obligations, property, possessions and succession. Although the first emperors created new laws by *senatus consultatum* (resolutions passed by the Senate), later emperors simply passed *constitutiones principium* (decrees). The emperor Justinian's *Codex constitutionum* of 529 CE collated all valid laws, and constitutes the basis of most of the legal systems in Western civilization.

The Tabula Claudina is the inscription in bronze of a speech given by the emperor Claudius in 48 CE. In his address to the Senate, the emperor recognized the right of the Gauls to be members of that ancient Roman institution.

hydraulic engineering, bridging and road-building. But more was involved than material factors. The Romans virtually founded town-planning as an art and administrative skill west of the Indus, and their inventions of concrete and the vaulted dome revolutionized the shapes of buildings. For the first time the interiors of buildings became more than a series of surfaces for decoration. Volumes and lighting became part of the subject-matter of architecture; the later Christian basilicas were to be the first great expressions of a new concern with the spaces inside buildings.

Roman technical accomplishment was stamped on an area stretching from the Black Sea in the east to Hadrian's Wall in the north and the Atlas mountains in the south. The capital, of course, contained some of its most spectacular relics. There, the wealth of empire

Roman roads

The Romans built 50,000 miles (80,000 km) of roads, constituting a transport network that united the most far-flung points of the empire. The majority of the routes, which were constructed mainly for military purposes, led to provincial cities that were islands of Graeco-Roman culture set in the middle of regions that had been scarcely romanized at all.

Roman roads were built to last: they had solid foundations topped with hard-wearing paving stones. Because the roads' surfaces were slightly higher in the middle than at the edges, water drained away – a feature that allowed the network to be relied on all year round. Many Roman roads were still in use during the Middle Ages.

expressed itself in a richness of finish and decoration nowhere else so concentrated. When the marble facings were intact, and paint and stucco moulding relieved the sheer mass of stone, Rome must have had some of the appeal to the imagination earlier possessed by Babylon. There was an ostentation about it which spoke of a certain vulgarity, too, and in this again it is not hard to sense a difference of quality between Rome and Greece; Roman civilization has a grossness and materiality inescapable in even its greatest monuments.

SOCIAL DIVISIONS

Roman materialism was, in part, the simple expression of the social realities on which the empire rested: Rome, like all the ancient

Many wealthy Romans lived in magnificent villas, expensively furnished and lavishly decorated. This mural adorned the bedroom wall of the Roman villa found at Boscoreale, just north of Pompeii. Dating from c.35 BCE, it depicts an idealized classical garden.

A Roman fresco depicting an urban villa. Of note is the elegant portico, which protected the villa's wealthy residents from the heat and the glare of the sun, as well as from the rain.

world, was built on a sharp division of rich and poor, and in the capital itself this division was an abyss not concealed but consciously expressed. The contrasts of wealth were flagrant in the difference between the sumptuousness of the houses of the new rich, drawing to themselves the profits of empire and calling on the services of perhaps scores of slaves on the spot and hundreds on the estates which maintained them, and the swarming tenements in which the Roman proletariat lived. Romans found no difficulty in accepting such divisions as part of the natural order; for that matter, few civilizations have ever much worried about them before our own, though few displayed them so flagrantly as imperial Rome. Unfortunately, though easy to recognize, the realities of wealth in Rome still remain curiously opaque to the historian. The finances of

only one senator, the younger Pliny, are known to us in any detail.

MUNICIPAL LIFE

The Roman pattern was reflected in all the great cities of the empire. It was central to the

The atrium, or vestibule, of a house was the main room. An opening in the roof provided light and a rectangular pond in the floor collected rain water, as can be seen in this house in Pompeii. Surrounding the atrium were the bedrooms. Luxurious homes such as this one would have belonged to wealthy families, while the majority of the urban population lived in tiny rooms in houses containing several apartments.

civilization which Rome sustained everywhere. The provincial cities stood like islands of Graeco-Roman culture in the aboriginal countrysides of the subject-peoples. Due allowance made for climate, they reflected a pattern of life of remarkable uniformity, displaying Roman priorities. Each had a forum, temples, a theatre, baths, whether added to old cities or built as part of the basic plan of those which were refounded. Regular grid-patterns were adopted as ground plans. The government of the cities was in the hands of local bigwigs, the *curiales* or city-fathers who at least until Trajan's time enjoyed a very large measure of independence in the conduct of municipal affairs, though later a tighter supervision was to be imposed on them. Some of these cities, such as Alexandria or Antioch, or Carthage (which the Romans refounded),

This portrait was found in Pompeii. It lay in the ruins between the houses of an aristocrat and a baker, which makes it difficult to establish the identities of the people portrayed. The writing boards and papyrus are symbols of a good education, suggesting that the figures are aristocrats, although their rustic appearance could also mean that they are commoners.

Martial on life in Rome

"Do you ask why I often visit my bit of land near dry Nomentum and my villa's dingy hearth? Sparsus, there's no place in Rome for a poor man to think or rest. Schoolmasters deny you life in the morning, bakers at night, the hammers of the coppersmiths all day. On one hand the idle money-changer rattles his grubby counter with Nero's metal, on the other the pounder of Spanish gold dust beats his well-worn stone with shining mallet; neither does Bellona's frenzied throng give up, nor the garrulous castaway with his swaddled trunk, nor the Jew that his mother taught to beg, nor the blear-eyed pedlar of sulphurated wares. Who can count up the losses of lazy sleep? He will tell us how many pots and pans the hands of the City clash when the moon is cut and beaten by the magic wheel of Colchis. You, Sparsus, know nothing of all this, nor can you know, leading your life of luxury in your Petilian domain, where your ground floor looks down on the hill tops ... where there's ... quiet that no tongues disturb, and no daylight save by admission. As for me, the thrusting of the passing crowd awakes me and Rome is at my bedside. Whenever I'm sick and tired of it and want to go to sleep, I go to my villa."

An extract from Book XII, v. 57, of the *Epigrams* by Martial (c.40–c.104 CE), translated by D. R. Shackleton Bailey.

grew to a very large size. The greatest of all cities was Rome itself, eventually containing more than a million people.

In this civilization the omnipresence of the amphitheatre is a standing reminder of the brutality and coarseness of which it was capable. It is important not to get this out of perspective, just as it is important not to infer too much about "decadence" from the much-quoted works of would-be moral reformers. One disadvantage under which the repute of Roman civilization has laboured is that it is one of the few before modern times in which we have very much insight into the popular

The Roman city

Roman civilization was centred on city life. In the provinces the Romans founded, or developed from existing nuclei, many imperial cities, where the political organizations and cultural activities for each province were based. Many of today's European cities have Roman origins, which are evident not only from the ruins that have been preserved but also from their street plans.

Typical Roman town plans are orthogonal in design, with two main axes and streets crossing each other at right angles. The origin of this type of plan is Greek, but evidence of the design can also be found in the ruins of Roman military encampments. Each city contained several open squares and various public buildings dedicated to religious, administrative or economic life, or to popular entertainment. Triumphal arches and gateways allowed access to the city, which was sometimes surrounded by fortified walls, particularly in the later stages of the empire, when the danger of attack from outside was very real.

Roman cities also had an advanced infrastructure. Water, for example, was carried to them via elaborate systems of pipes and aqueducts and then stored in central reserves, from which water supplies were distributed. At the end of the 3rd century CE, Rome had 11 free public baths and more than 800 private ones. (The Caracalla Baths, which were opened in 216 CE by the emperor Caracalla himself, could accommodate up to 1,600 bathers.) Many Roman cities even had sewerage networks.

From the 4th century CE onwards, Rome's Caracalla Baths fell into disuse and were eventually dismantled to provide stone for other buildings, reducing them to their present state (above).

mind through its entertainments, for the gladiatorial games and the wild-beast shows were emphatically mass entertainment in a way in which the Greek theatre was not. Popular relaxation is in any era hardly likely to be found edifying by the sensitive, and the Romans institutionalized its least attractive aspects by building great centres for their shows, and by permitting the mass-entertainment industry to be used as a political device; the provision of spectacular games was one of the ways in which a rich man could bring to bear his wealth to secure political advancement. Nevertheless, when all allowances are made for the fact that we cannot know how, say, the ancient masses of Egypt or Assyria amused themselves, we are left with the uniqueness of the gladiatorial spectacle; it was an exploitation of cruelty as entertainment on a bigger scale than ever before and one unrivalled until the twentieth-century cinema. It was made possible by the urbanization of Roman culture, which could deliver larger mass audiences than ever. The ultimate roots of the "games" were Etruscan, but their development sprang from a new scale of urbanism and the exigencies of Roman politics.

Public entertainment

The inhabitants of Roman cities often enjoyed free entertainment, paid for by local dignataries, senators or sometimes the emperor himself. For the sponsors, staging public performances in theatres, amphi-theatres or circuses was a method of demonstrating their wealth and social prestige and increasing their popularity.

The performances that the Romans loved best were the gladiator fights, the wild animal fights and the chariot races. Success or failure in the games could be a matter of life or death for the participants – these were often exceptionally cruel and bloody spectacles. Even outside the arena, rivalry between supporters of opposing individuals or teams could frequently lead to violent confrontations.

These terracotta figurines represent two gladiators in combat. Most gladiators were prisoners of war or convicts condemned to death; some were free men who were paid to fight. They underwent gruelling training at Rome's imperial school of gladiators.

Although, to modern-day students of Roman civilization, this use of violence for the entertainment of the masses may seem horrible, the games played a very important part in city life in the empire. They served as a powerful outlet for social tensions and instilled a sense of cultural identity. The free food that was often distributed during the perfor-mances also went some way to lessening the misery of the urban poor.

Chariot racing was the oldest kind of public performance. Races took place in the circuses, and the participating teams of charioteers were distinguished from each other by the colour of their clothes. This detail from a 4th-century mosaic, from a villa near Barcelona, shows a quadriga *(a chariot drawn by four horses). Several important centres for the breeding and exportation of horses were located in Hispania (Spain) towards the end of the imperial era.*

Although, owing to an economic crisis, it was never finished, this amphitheatre in El Djem (Tunisia) was the largest in the Roman province of Africa. Built at the beginning of the 3rd century CE, its structure and decoration are based on Rome's Colosseum.

SLAVERY

Another aspect of the brutality at the heart of Roman society was, of course, far from unique: the omnipresence of slavery. As in Greek society, it was so varied in its expression that it cannot be summarized in a generalization. Many slaves earned wages, some bought their freedom, and the Roman slave had rights at law. The growth of large plantation estates, it is true, provided examples of a new intensification of it in the first century or so, but it would be hard to say Roman slavery was worse than that of other ancient societies. A few who questioned the institution were very untypical: moralists reconciled themselves to slave-owning as easily as later Christians.

RELIGION

Much of what we know about popular mentality before modern times is known through religion. Roman religion was a very obvious part of Roman life, but that may be misleading if we think in modern terms. It had nothing to do with individual salvation and not much with individual behaviour; it was above all a public matter. It was a part of the *res publica*, a series of rituals whose maintenance was good for the state, whose neglect would bring retribution. There was no priestly caste set apart from other people (if we exclude one or two

This 1st-century funerary bas-relief is from the tomb of a slave couple who had gained their freedom – denoted by the letter L (*libertus*) written after their names. The fact that they are depicted holding hands confirms that their marriage was recognized by law.

The Temple of Hadrian in Ephesus in Asia Minor was founded in the 2nd century CE by a local noble family. On the façade, two pilasters frame columns crowned with Corinthian capitals. The cornice would have continued in an arch and would have been finished off by a triangular pediment, now lost. In the keystone of the arch is an image of the goddess of Ephesus.

antiquarian survivals in the temples of a few special cults) and priestly duties were the task of the magistrates, who found priesthood a useful social and political lever. Nor was there creed or dogma. What was required of Romans was only that the ordained services and rituals should be carried out in the accustomed way; for proletarians this meant little except that they should not work on a holiday. The civic authorities were everywhere responsible for the rites, as they were responsible for the maintenance of the temples. The proper observances had a powerfully practical purpose: Livy reports a consul saying the gods "look kindly on the scrupulous observance of religious rites which has brought our country to its peak". People genuinely felt that the peace of Augustus was the *Pax deorum*, a divine reward for a proper respect

for the gods which Augustus had reasserted. Somewhat more cynically, Cicero had remarked that the gods were needed to prevent chaos in society. This, if different, was also an expression of the Roman's practical approach to religion. It was not insincere or disbelieving; the recourse to diviners for the interpretation of omens and the acceptance of the decisions of the augurs about important acts of policy would alone establish that. But it was unmysterious and down-to-earth in its understanding of the official cults.

RELIGIOUS CULTS

The content of the official cults was a mixture of Greek mythology and festivals and rites derived from primitive Roman practice and therefore heavily marked by agricultural preoccupations. One which lived to deck itself out in the symbols of another religion was the December Saturnalia, which is with us still as Christmas. But the religion practised by Romans stretched far beyond official rites. The most striking feature of the Roman approach to religion was its eclecticism and cosmopolitanism. There was room in the empire for all manner of belief, provided it did not contravene public order or inhibit adherence to the official observances. For the most part, the peasants everywhere pursued the timeless superstitions of their local nature cults, townspeople took up new crazes from time to time, and the educated professed some acceptance of the classical pantheon of Greek gods and led the people in the official observances. Each clan and household, finally, sacrificed to its own god with appropriate special rituals at the great moments of human life: childbirth, marriage, sickness and death. Each household had its shrine, each street-corner its idol.

THE IMPERIAL CULT

Under Augustus there was a deliberate attempt to reinvigorate old belief, which had been somewhat eroded by closer acquaintance with the Hellenistic East and about which a few sceptics had shown cynicism even in the second century BCE. After Augustus, emperors always held the office of chief priest (*pontifex maximus*) and political and religious primacy were thus combined in the same person. This began the increasing importance and definition of the imperial cult itself. It fitted well the Romans' innate conservatism, their respect for the ways and customs of their ancestors. The imperial cult linked respect for traditional patrons, the placating or invoking of familiar deities and the commemoration of outstanding personalities and events, to the ideas of divine kingship which came from the East, from Asia. It was there that altars were first raised to Rome or the Senate, and there that they were soon reattributed to the emperor. The

Built at the end of the 2nd century BCE, the circular temple of Hercules Victor is the oldest marble temple in Rome. Although it was consecrated to Hercules, it is often called the Temple of Vesta because it once housed the sacred fire of Vesta, goddess of the household.

This 1st-century CE statue represents Claudius as the god Jupiter, emphasizing the emperor's unlimited power and magnifying his glory.

This detail from a bas-relief shows a great sacrificial procession, part of festivities that were held in memory of the emperor Augustus during the 1st century CE. The figures in the foreground are *ministri*, slaves specially chosen to carry small statues of the *lares* gods.

cult spread through the whole empire, though it was not until the third century CE that the practice was wholly respectable at Rome itself, so strong was republican sentiment. But even there the strains of empire had already favoured a revival of official piety which benefited the imperial cult.

EXTERNAL INFLUENCES

The deification of rulers was not the only external influence that came from the East. By the second century, the distinction of a pure Roman religious tradition from others within the empire is virtually impossible. The Roman pantheon, like the Greek, was absorbed almost indistinguishably into a mass of beliefs and cults, their boundaries blurred and fluid, merging imperceptibly over a scale of experience running from sheer

magic to the philosophical monotheism popularized by the stoic philosophies. The intellectual and religious world of the empire was omnivorous, credulous and deeply irrational. It is important here not to be over-impressed by the visible practicality of the Roman mind; practical people are often superstitious. Nor was the Greek heritage understood in an altogether rational way; its philosophers were seen by the first century BCE as men inspired, holy men whose mystical teaching was the most eagerly studied part of their works, and even Greek civilization had always rested on a broad basis of popular superstition and local cult practice. Tribal gods swarmed throughout the Roman world.

All this boils down to a large measure of practical criticism of the ancient Roman ways. Obviously, they were no longer enough for an urban civilization, however numerically preponderant the peasants on which it rested. Many of the traditional festivals were pastoral or agricultural in origin, but occasionally even the god they invoked was forgotten. City-dwellers gradually came to need more than piety in a more and more puzzling world. People grasped desperately at anything which could give meaning to the world and some degree of control over it. Old superstitions and new crazes benefited. The evidence can be seen in the appeal of the Egyptian gods, whose cults flooded through the empire as its security made travel and intercourse easier (they were even patronized by an

Roman soldiers first came into contact with the Persian god Mithras in Asia Minor. The Mithraic cult, which offered hope of life after death, became immensely popular in the Roman army and quickly spread throughout the empire. This sculpture represents Mithras killing the bull from whose blood the life of the universe flows.

emperor, the Libyan Septimius Severus). A civilized world of greater complexity and unity than any earlier was also one of greater and greater religiosity and a curiousness almost boundless. One of the last great teachers of pagan antiquity, Apollonius of Tyana, was said to have lived and studied with the *Brahmans* of India. Men and women were looking about for new saviours long before one was found in the first century CE.

MYSTERY CULTS

Another symptom of Eastern influence was the popularization of mysteries, cults which rested upon the communication of special virtues and powers to the initiated by secret rites. The sacrificial cult of Mithras, a minor Zoroastrian deity especially favoured by soldiers, was one of the most famous. Almost all the mysteries register impatience with the constraints of the material world, an ultimate pessimism about it and a preoccupation with (and perhaps a promise of survival after) death. In this lay their power to provide a psychological satisfaction no longer offered by the old gods and never really possessed by the official cult. They drew individuals to them; they had the appeal that was later to draw converts to Christianity, which in its earliest days was often seen, significantly, as another mystery.

UNREST IN THE EMPIRE

That Roman rule did not satisfy all Roman subjects all the time was even true in Italy itself as late as 73 BCE when, in the disorderly last age of the republic, a great slave revolt required three years of military campaigning and was punished with the crucifixion of 6,000 slaves along the roads from Rome to

This detail from a 1st-century BCE painting is from the Villa of the Mysteries in Pompeii. The woman wearing a veil is acting as an initiator in a Dionysiac mystic ritual. Initiation ceremonies for various cults, including Mithraism, took place throughout the Mediterranean region during the Hellenistic era. Only the initiated were allowed to know the cults' "mysteries", or secrets, hence the label. Mystic rituals were banned in Rome, on the grounds of the extreme emotional state to which the participants were often reduced and because of the leaders' alleged excesses. But the rituals continued in secret celebrations shrouded in an aura of religious fervour, prohibition and occultism.

Roman religion

Traditional Roman religion was essentially a combination of rituals performed either publicly by representatives of the state or privately by the members of a family. The relationship between the gods and human beings was considered to be a kind of contract – Romans fulfilled their obligations, by performing rituals and offering sacrifices, in the hope that the gods would fulfill theirs, by providing protection and good fortune.

Roman gods adopted the human form in the 3rd century BCE, when Rome incorporated the Greek pantheon. The divinities of Hellenic origin that received the most attention were the Capitoline Triad, consisting of Jupiter (the Greek Zeus), Juno (Hera) and Minerva (Athene). In private religion, the *penates* (household gods), the *lares* (ancestors' spirits) and the goddess Vesta were revered.

After the conquest of Greece, philosophers and intellectuals from around the Hellenistic world arrived in Rome. Especially popular amongst the masses were the religious mysteries dedicated to Dionysus, Cybele, Isis and Osiris, and Mithras. These cults shared similar initiation rights and the belief that a judgment after death would decide whether the deceased was to be saved or damned.

Rome's domed Pantheon, which is among the buildings represented by this model, was constructed in the 1st century BCE as a temple dedicated to all the Roman gods.

the south. In the provinces revolt was endemic, always likely to be provoked by a particular burst of harsh or bad government. Such was the famous rebellion of Boadicea in Britain, or the earlier Pannonian revolt under Augustus. Sometimes such troubles could look back to local traditions of independence, as was the case at Alexandria where they were frequent. In one particular instance, that of the Jews, they touched chords not unlike those of later nationalism. The spectacular Jewish record of disobedience and resistance goes back beyond Roman rule to 170 BCE, when they bitterly resisted the "westernizing" practices of the Hellenistic kingdoms which first adumbrated policies later to be taken up by Rome. The imperial cult made matters worse. Even Jews who did not mind Roman tax-gatherers and thought that Caesar should have rendered unto him what was Caesar's were bound to draw the line at the blasphemy of sacrifice at his altar. In 66 CE came a great revolt; there were others under Trajan and Hadrian. Jewish communities were powder-barrels. Their sensitivity makes somewhat more understandable the unwillingness of a procurator of Judaea in about 30 CE to press hard for the strict observance of the legal rights of an accused man when Jewish leaders demanded his death.

TAXATION AND THE ECONOMY

Taxes kept the empire going. Although not heavy in normal times, when they paid for administration and police quite comfortably, they were a hated burden and one augmented, too, from time to time, by levies in kind, requisitioning and forced recruiting. For a long time, they drew on a prosperous and growing economy. This was not only a matter of such lucky imperial acquisitions as the gold-mines of Dacia. The growth in the circulation of trade and the stimulus provided by the new markets of the great frontier encampments also favoured the appearance of new industry and suppliers. The huge numbers of wine jars found by archaeologists are only an indicator of what must have been a vast commerce – of foodstuffs, textiles, spices – which have left fewer traces. Yet the economic base of empire was always agriculture. This was not rich by modern standards, for its techniques were primitive; no Roman farmer ever saw a windmill and watermills were still rare when the empire ended in the West. For all its idealization, rural life was a harsh and laborious thing. To it too, therefore, the *Pax Romana* was essential: it meant that taxes could be found from the small surplus produced and that lands would not be ravaged.

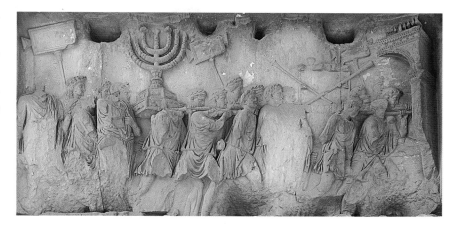

THE ROLE OF THE ARMY IN THE ROMAN STATE

In the last resort almost everything seems to come back to the army, on which the Roman peace depended; yet it was an instrument which changed over six centuries as much as did the Roman state itself. Roman society and

This bas-relief from the arch of Titus celebrates the emperor's conquest of Judaea in the year 70 CE. The scene represents a procession of Roman soldiers carrying spoils from the destroyed Temple of Jerusalem.

Judaism in the ancient world

Jewish communities have existed in a number of European cities since ancient times, when there were large Jewish populations in the eastern Mediterranean, to the north of Gaul and along the Rhine.

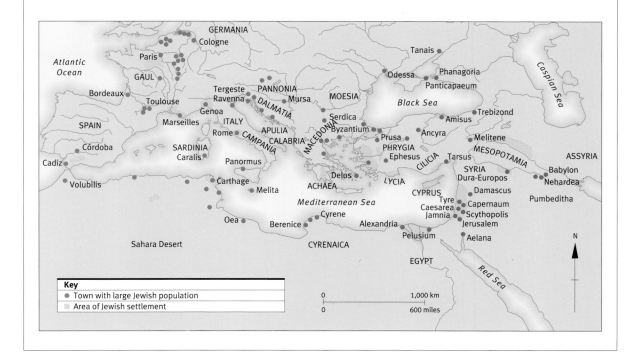

Key
- Town with large Jewish population
- Area of Jewish settlement

0   1,000 km
0   600 miles

These amphoras, which were used for the transportation of wine, are from a trade vessel found in a Ligurian port. Wine was an indispensable part of the Roman diet and an important commercial product. Together with oil, it had to be transported from the Mediterranean countries to all the parts of the empire where Roman legions were stationed.

culture were always militaristic, yet the instruments of that militarism changed. From the time of Augustus the army was a regular long-service force, no longer relying even formally upon the obligation of all citizens to serve. The ordinary legionary served for twenty years, four in reserve, and he more and more came from the provinces as time went by. Surprising as it may seem, given the repute of Roman discipline, volunteers seem to have been plentiful enough for letters of recommendation and the use of patrons to be resorted to by would-be recruits. The twenty-eight legions which were the normal establishment after the defeat in Germany were distributed along the frontiers, about 160,000 men in all. They were the core of the army, which contained about as many men again in the cavalry, auxiliaries and other arms. The legions continued to be commanded by senators (except in Egypt) and the central issue of politics at the capital itself was still access to opportunities such as this. For, as had become clearer and clearer as the centuries passed, it was in the camps of the legions that the heart of the empire lay, though the Praetorian Guard at Rome sometimes contested their right to choose an emperor. Yet the soldiers made only part of the history of the empire. Quite as much impact was made on it, in the long run, by the handful of men who were the followers and disciples of the man the procurator of Judaea had handed over to execution.

A group of Praetorian soldiers is depicted in this marble bas-relief from the 2nd century CE. The Praetorian Guard was created by Augustus to maintain public order and enforce the law. Its most important duty was to protect the person of the emperor, upon whom it was dependent.

3 JEWRY AND THE COMING OF CHRISTIANITY

This mosaic from the 6th-century CE church of Saints Cosmas and Damian in Rome depicts Christ as the Pantocrator (a Byzantine term meaning omnipotent God).

FEW READERS OF THIS BOOK are likely to have heard of Abgar, far less of his east Syrian kingdom, Osrhoene; both were unknown to the writer until he was well embarked upon this book. Yet this little-known and obscure monarch is a landmark: he was long believed to be the first Christian king. In fact, the story of his conversion is a legend; it seems to have been under his descendant, Abgar VIII (or IX, so vague is our information), that Osrhoene became Christian at the end of the second century CE. The conversion may not even have included the king himself, but this did not trouble hagiographers. They placed Abgar at the head of a long and great tradition; in the end it was to incorporate virtually the whole history of monarchy in Europe. From there, in turn, it was to spread to influence rulers in other parts of the world.

THE IMPACT OF CHRISTIANITY

All these later monarchs would behave differently because they saw themselves as Christian, yet, important though it was, this is only a tiny part of the difference Christianity has made to history. Until the coming of industrial society, in fact, it is the only historical phenomenon we have to consider whose implications, creative power and impact are comparable with the great determinants of prehistory in shaping the world we live in. Christianity grew up within the classical world of the Roman Empire, fusing itself in the end with its institutions and spreading through its social and mental structures to become our most important legacy from that civilization. Often disguised or muted, its influence runs through all the great creative processes of the last fifteen hundred years; almost incidentally, it defined Europe. We are what we are today because a handful of Jews saw their teacher and leader crucified and believed he rose again from the dead.

CHRISTIANITY'S JEWISH ORIGINS

THE JEWISHNESS of Christianity is fundamental and was probably its salvation (to speak in purely human terms), for the odds against the historical survival, let alone worldwide success, of a small sect centred upon a holy man in the Roman Eastern Empire were enormous. Judaism was a matrix and protecting environment for a long time as well as the source of the most fundamental Christian ideas. In return, Jewish ideas and myths were to be generalized through Christianity to become world forces. At the heart of these was the Jewish view that history was a meaningful story, providentially ordained, a cosmic drama of the unfolding design of the one, omnipotent God for His chosen people. Through His covenant with that people could be found guidance for right action, and it lay in adherence to His law. The breaking of that law had always brought punishment; it had come to the whole people in the deserts of Sinai and by the waters of Babylon. This great drama was the inspiration of Jewish historical writing, in which the Jews of the Roman Empire discerned the pattern which made their lives meaningful.

JEWISH HISTORY

That very relevant mythological pattern was deeply rooted in Jewish historical experience, which, after the great days of Solomon, had been bitter, fostering an enduring distrust of the foreigner and an iron will to survive. Few things are in fact more remarkable in the life of this remarkable people than the simple fact of its continued existence. The Exile which began in 587 BCE when Babylonian conquerors took many of the Jews away after the destruction of the Temple was the last crucial experience in the moulding of their national identity before modern times. It finally crystallized the Jewish vision of history. The exiles heard prophets like Ezekiel promise a renewed covenant; Judah had been punished for her sins by exile and the Temple's destruction, now God would turn His face again to her, she would return again to Jerusalem, delivered out of Babylon as Israel had been delivered out of Ur, out of Egypt. The Temple would be rebuilt. Perhaps only a minority of the Jews of the Exile

The Dura-Europos synagogue was built c.200 BCE. These remarkably well-preserved frescoes from the synagogue's walls depict scenes from the Hebrew Bible.

Time chart (587 BCE–70 CE)

				26–36 CE Governorship of Pontius Pilate, during which Christ dies		66–70 CE Jewish uprising against Rome	
	538 BCE Exiled Jews return to Jerusalem						
600 BCE	500 BCE	50 BCE	0	25 CE	50 CE	75 CE	
	587 BCE Destruction of Jerusalem by Babylonians	63 BCE Pompey imposes Roman rule on Judaea	37–4 BCE Reign of Herod the Great, during which Christ is thought to have been born		49 CE Apostolic Council of Jerusalem		

heeded this, but it was a large one and it included Judah's religious and administrative élite, if we are to judge by the quality of those – again, probably a minority – who, when they could do so, returned to Jerusalem, a saving Remnant, according to prophecy.

THE JEWS IN EXILE

Before the return to Jerusalem, the experience of the Exile had transformed Jewish life as well as confirming the Jewish vision. Scholars are divided as to whether the more important developments took place among the exiles or among the Jews who were left in Judah to lament what had happened. In one way or another, though, Jewish religious life was deeply stirred. The most important change was the implanting of the reading of the scriptures as the central act of Jewish religion. While the Old Testament was not to assume its final form for another three or four centuries, the first five books, or "Pentateuch", traditionally ascribed to Moses, were substantially complete soon after the return from the Exile. Without the focus of cult practice at the Temple the Jews seem to have turned to weekly meetings to hear these sacred texts

The Muslim sanctuary of Nebi Musain in the Jordan valley stands on the site that Muslims believe to be the final resting place of Moses.

Jewish themes often appear in early Christian art. This 4th-century CE mural, from the Via Latina catacomb in Rome, represents Jacob and his children arriving in Egypt.

read and expounded. They contained the promise of a future and guidance to its achievement through maintenance of the Law, now given a new detail and coherence. This was one of the slow effects of the work of the interpreters and scribes who had to reconcile and explain the sacred books. In the end there was to grow out of these weekly meetings both the institution of the synagogue and a new liberation of religion from locality and ritual, however much and long Jews continued to pine for the restoration of the Temple. The Jewish religion could eventually be practised wherever Jews could come together to read the scriptures; they were to be the first of the peoples of a Book, and Christians and Muslims were to follow them. It made possible greater abstraction and universalizing of the vision of God.

There were narrowings, too. Although

Jewish religion might be separated from the Temple cult, some prophets had seen the redemption and purification which must lie ahead as only to be approached through an even more rigid enforcement of what was now believed to be Mosaic law. Ezra brought back its precepts from Babylon and observances which had been in origin those of nomads were now imposed rigorously on an increasingly urbanized people. The self-segregation of Jews became much more important and obvious in towns; it was seen as a part of the purification which was needed that every Jew married to a gentile wife (and there must have been many) should divorce her.

INDEPENDENCE AND REVOLT

After the Persian overthrow of Babylon in 538 BCE some of the Jews took the opportunity offered to them and came back to Jerusalem. The Temple was rebuilt and Judah became under Persian overlordship a sort of theocratic satrapy, effective administrative power being in the hands of the priestly aristocracy, which provided the political articulation of Jewish nationhood until Roman times.

With the ending of Persian rule, the age of Alexander's heirs brought new problems. After being ruled by the Ptolemies, the Jews eventually passed to the Seleucids. The social behaviour and thinking of the upper classes underwent the influence of Hellenization; this sharpened divisions by exaggerating contrasts of wealth and differences between townspeople and country dwellers. It also separated the priestly families from the people, who remained firmly in the tradition of

Judaism was not the Near East's only religion. This fresco, c.75 BCE, is from the temple of the Palmyran gods in Dura-Europos; it depicts the cult's priests.

the Law and the Prophets, as expounded in the synagogues. It was against a king of Hellenistic Syria, Antiochus IV, and cultural "westernization" approved by the priests, but resented as have been such processes in modern times by the masses, that the great Maccabaean revolt broke out (168–164 BCE). Antiochus had tried to go too fast; not content with the steady erosion of Jewish insularity by Hellenistic civilization and the friction of example, he had interfered with Jewish rites and profaned the Temple. After the revolt had been repressed with difficulty (and guerrilla war went on long after), a more conciliatory policy was resumed by the

Antiochus IV, the Seleucid king of Syria, is depicted on this coin. He transformed Solomon's Temple in Jerusalem into a Greek sanctuary, provoking the Maccabaean revolt.

The beliefs of Judaism

The term Judaism refers to the religious tradition of the Jewish people, whose most ancient texts are those collected in the Hebrew Bible, or the Christian Bible's Old Testament. In accordance with biblical tradition, the basic idea of the Covenant between the god Yahweh and his people was determined in the time of Moses, the legendary patriarch who is thought to have lived in the 13th century BCE. Exclusive loyalty to Yahweh was the feature that distinguished the Jews from the polytheistic peoples among whom they lived. Yahweh was the all-powerful eternal god, creator of all things. He was a strictly fair god, who brought death to the impious and destroyed his enemies but had mercy on the faithful. He severely punished those who disobeyed his laws, but was also the loving and compassionate father of his chosen people, the Jews, to whom he had promised to send a Messiah who would lead them to victory against their enemies.

From the 8th century BCE, successive prophets affirmed the belief that the misfortunes of Israel, including its subjection to foreign conquerors, were a punishment from Yahweh for not having honoured the Covenant. They also stated, however, that Israel's sufferings would purify the Jews and prepare them for future glory, which would culminate in Yahweh being recognized by all the world's peoples.

The Jews' loss of independence and their subjection to successive empires (Persian, Macedonian and Roman) led to the growth of nuclei of Jewish exiles in various parts of the Mediterranean and the Near East: this process of dispersal was known as the *diaspora*, literally meaning "scattering". In Palestine itself, the Jewish presence was practically eliminated following the failure of the nationalist revolts against Rome in the 1st and 2nd centuries CE, but, under the guidance of the rabbis, Judaism would survive the diaspora. At the beginning of the 3rd century CE, the oral tradition of Jewish law was set down in the Mishna, which later became the first part of the Talmud, the body of Jewish law and legend.

Seleucid kings. It did not satisfy many Jews, who in 142 BCE were able to take advantage of a favourable set of circumstances to win an independence which was to last for nearly eighty years. Then, in 63 BCE, Pompey imposed Roman rule and there disappeared the last independent Jewish state in the Near East for nearly two thousand years.

Independence had not been a happy experience. A succession of kings drawn from the priestly families had thrown the country into disorder by innovation and high-handedness. They and the priests who acquiesced in their policies excited opposition. They were challenged in their authority by a new, more austere school of interpreters, who clung to the Law, rather than the cult, as the heart of Judaism and gave it new and searchingly rigorous interpretation. These were the Pharisees, the representatives of a reforming strain which was time and time again to express itself in Jewry in protest against the danger of creeping Hellenization. They also accepted proselytism among non-Jews, teaching a belief in the resurrection of the dead and a divine Last Judgment; there was a mixture in their stance of national and universal aspiration and they drew out further the implications of Jewish monotheism.

THE SPREAD OF JUDAISM

Most of the Pharisees' activity took place in Judaea, the tiny rump of the once great kingdom of David; fewer Jews lived there in the time of Augustus than in the rest of the empire. From the seventh century onwards they had spread over the civilized world. The armies of Egypt, Alexander and the Seleucids all had Jewish regiments. Others had settled abroad in the course of trade. One of the greatest Jewish colonies was at Alexandria, where they had gathered from about 300 BCE. The Alexandrian Jews were Greek-speakers; there the Old Testament was first translated into Greek and when Jesus was born there were probably more Jews there than in Jerusalem. At Rome there were approximately another 50,000. Such agglomerations increased the opportunities to proselytize and therefore the danger of friction between communities.

THE ATTRACTIONS OF JUDAISM

Judaism offered much to a world in which traditional cults had waned. Circumcision and dietary restraints were obstacles, but were far outweighed for many a proselyte by the attractions of a code of behaviour of great minuteness, a form of religion not dependent on temples, shrines or priesthood for its exercise, and, above all, the assurance of salvation. A prophet whose teaching was ascribed by the Old Testament compilers to Isaiah, but who is almost certainly of the Exile, had already announced a message to bring light to the gentiles, and many of them had responded to that light long before the Christians, who were to promote it in a special sense. The proselytes could identify themselves with the Chosen People in the great story which inspired Jewish historical writing, the only achievement in this field worthy of comparison with the Greek invention of scientific history, and one which gave meaning to the tragedies of the world. In their history the Jews discerned an unfolding pattern by which they were being refined in the fire for the Day of Judgment. A fundamental contribution of Judaism to Christianity would be its sense of the people apart, its eyes set on things not of this world; Christians were to go on to the idea of the leaven in the

lump, working to redeem the world. Both myths were deeply rooted in Jewish historical experience and in the remarkable though simple fact of this people's survival at all.

THE JEWS UNDER ROMAN RULE

The big communities of Jews and Jewish proselytes were important social facts to Roman governors, standing out not only because of their size but because of their tenacious separateness. Archaeological evidence of synagogues as distinct and separate buildings does not appear until well into the Common Era, but Jewish quarters in cities were distinct, clustering about their own synagogues and courts of law. While proselytizing was widespread and even some Romans were attracted by Jewish belief, there were also early signs of popular dislike of Jews at Rome itself. Rioting was frequent in Alexandria and easily spread to other towns of the Near East. This led to distrust on the part of authorities and (at least at Rome) to the dispersal of Jewish communities when things became difficult.

The Bible contains several stories about the extraordinary protection that Yahweh was believed to offer his followers. One of the best known is that of the three young Jews who were thrown into a burning oven by King Nebuchadnezzar for refusing to prostrate themselves before his statue. This 3rd-century CE mural painting from the Priscilla catacomb in Rome depicts the three Jews emerging from the oven unhurt.

Jerusalem

Though little of what he did survives, Herod the Great (74–4 BCE), who was put on the throne of Judaea by the Romans in 37 BCE, constructed many buildings in Jerusalem. In particular, he began work to rebuild the Temple – a project that took 46 years to complete – including raising it on a huge platform and adding the Temple square, where money-lenders and merchants could do business. Herod also constructed a new fortress, Antonia, to protect the Temple.

Between 66 and 74 CE, the Jews rebelled against Roman rule in the Judaean War. In March 70 CE the Roman army laid siege to Jerusalem, and the two outer city walls fell in May. Four months later, the Romans broke through the inner defences. They devastated the city, killing or enslaving its inhabitants and destroying the Temple, more than six centuries after the Babylonians' destruction, in 587 BCE, of the first Temple, built by Solomon on the same spot. Only the western wall (or Wailing Wall) of the Temple platform remains today.

Key
▤ Reigns of David and Solomon, 10th century BCE
▤ Hasmonean period, 2nd century BCE
▤ Older construction, restored and added to by Herod the Great
▤ Reign of Herod the Great, 40–4 BCE

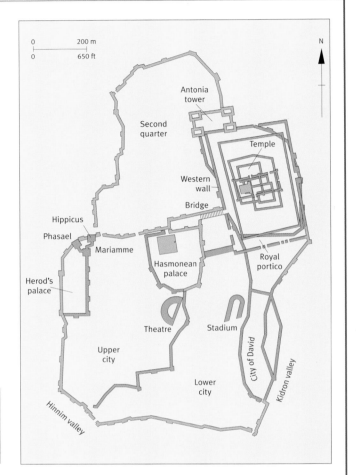

A plan of Jerusalem (top) in the time of Herod the Great, and a view of the city today (above), looking westwards. The walls in the foreground follow those of the Temple platform built by Herod the Great. On the right is the Dome of the Rock – a 7th-century CE mosque built on the site of Solomon's Temple and the third most holy place in Islam.

KING HEROD

Judaea itself was regarded as a particularly ticklish and dangerous area and to this the religious ferment of the last century and a half BCE had greatly contributed. In 37 BCE the Senate appointed a Jew, Herod the Great, King of Judaea. He was an unpopular monarch. No doubt this was in part a matter of national distaste for a Roman nominee and a ruler anxious – with reason – to preserve the friendship of Rome, but it was exacerbated by the Hellenistic style of life at his court (though he was careful to display his loyalty to the Jewish religion) and by the heavy taxes which he raised, some of them for grandiose building. Even if it were not for the legendary Massacre of the Innocents and his place in Christian demonology, Herod would not have had a good historical press. At his death, in 4 BCE, his kingdom was divided between his three sons, an unsatisfactory arrangement which was superseded in 6 CE, when Judaea became part of the Roman province of Syria governed from Caesarea. In 26 CE Pontius Pilate became procurator, or governor, and was to hold the uncomfortable and exacting post for ten years.

JEWISH UNREST

The end of the first century BCE was a bad moment in the history of a turbulent province. Something of a climax to the excitements of nearly two centuries was being reached. The Jews were at loggerheads with their Samaritan neighbours and resented an influx of Greek-Syrians noticeable in the coastal towns. They detested Rome as the latest of a long line of conquerors and also because of its demands for taxes; tax-gatherers – the "publicans" of the New Testament – were unpopular not just because of what they took but because they took it for the foreigner. But worse still, the Jews were also bitterly divided between themselves. The great religious festivals were often

Herodium, the citadel that Herod the Great built close to Jerusalem, is seen in this aerial view. Herod was buried in his citadel in 4 BCE, which, according to most modern historians, was shortly after the birth of Christ.

In caves at Qumran, close to the Dead Sea, 1st-century BCE scrolls have been found. The scrolls, some of which had been preserved in urns such as this one, are thought to have been written by members of the Jewish ascetic community of the Essenes.

stained by bloodshed and rioting. Pharisees, for instance, were bitterly divided from Sadducees, the formalizing representatives of the aristocratic priestly caste. Other sects rejected them both. One of the most interesting of them has become known to us only in recent years, through the discovery and reading of the Dead Sea Scrolls, in which it can be seen to have promised its adherents much that was also the promise of early Christianity. It looked forward to a last deliverance which would follow Judaea's apostasy and would be announced by the coming of a Messiah. Jews attracted by such teaching searched the writings of the Prophets for the prefigurings of these things. Others sought a more direct way. The Zealots looked to the nationalist resistance movement as the way ahead.

JESUS OF NAZARETH

INTO THIS ELECTRIC ATMOSPHERE Jesus was born in about 6 BCE, into a world in which thousands of his countrymen awaited the coming of a Messiah, a leader who would lead them to military or symbolic victory and inaugurate the last and greatest days of Jerusalem. The evidence for the facts of his life is contained in the records written down after his death in the Gospels, the assertions and traditions which the early Church based on the testimony of those who had actually known Jesus. The Gospels are not by themselves satisfactory evidence but their inadequacies can be exaggerated. They were no doubt written to demonstrate the supernatural authority of Jesus and the confirmation provided by the events of his life for

This is one of the Dead Sea Scrolls that were found at Qumran. It reproduces a fragment of the Bible from the Book of Isaiah.

the prophecies which had long announced the coming of Messiah. This interested and hagiographical origin does not demand scepticism about all the facts asserted; many have inherent plausibility in that they are what might be expected of a Jewish religious leader of the period. They need not be rejected; much more inadequate evidence about far more intractable subjects has often to be employed. There is no reason to be more austere or rigorous in our canons of acceptability for early Christian records than for, say, the evidence in Homer which illuminates Mycenae. Nevertheless, it is very hard to find corroborative evidence of the facts stated in the Gospels in other records.

THE GOSPELS' STORY OF JESUS

The picture of Jesus presented in the Gospels is of a man of modest though not destitute family, with a claim to royal lineage. Such a claim would no doubt have been denied by his opponents if there had not been

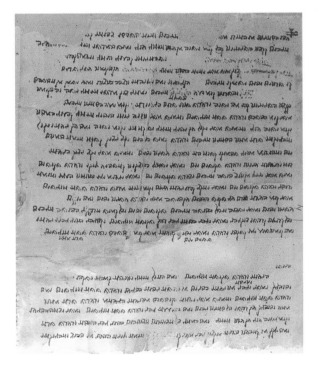

This mosaic, which embellishes the central dome of the Neonian baptistry in Ravenna, dates from the 5th century CE. John the Baptist is shown baptizing Christ, who is immersed in the waters, in the presence of the Holy Spirit.

something in it. Galilee, where Jesus grew up, was something of a frontier area for Judaism, where it was most exposed to the contact with Greek-Syrians which often irritated religious sensibilities. There preached in the neighbourhood a man called John, a prophet to whom crowds had flocked in the days before his arrest and execution. Scholars now believe John to have been connected with the Qumran community which left behind the Dead Sea Scrolls. One evangelist tells us that

he was the cousin of Jesus; this is possibly true, but less important than the agreement of all the Gospels that John baptized Jesus as he baptized countless others who came to him fearing the approach of the Last Day. He is also said to have recognized in Jesus a teacher like himself and perhaps something more: "Art thou He that cometh, or look we for another?" Jesus knew himself to be a holy man; his teaching and the evidence of his sanctity which was seen in miracles soon convinced the excited multitude to Jerusalem. His triumphal entry to the city was based on their spontaneous feeling. They followed him as they followed other great teachers in the hope of the Messiah that was to come. The end was a charge of blasphemy before the Jewish court and the relaxation of the letter of Roman law by a Roman governor in order to avoid further trouble in a violent city. Jesus was not a Roman citizen and for such men the extreme penalty was crucifixion after scourging. The inscription on the cross on which he was nailed said: "Jesus of Nazareth, King of the Jews"; this made clear that a political act was envisaged; and that the significance of it should not go unmissed was ensured by posting the inscription in Latin, Greek and Hebrew. This was probably in 33 CE, though 29 CE and 30 CE have also been put forward as dates. Shortly after his death, Jesus' disciples believed that he had risen from the dead, that they had seen him and his ascension into heaven, and that they had received a divine gift of power from him at Pentecost which should sustain them and their adherents until the Last Day. That would soon come, they also believed, and would bring back Jesus as the judge sitting at the right hand of God. All this the Gospels tell us.

The Sermon on the Mount

"And seeing the multitudes, he went up into a mountain, and when he had sat, his disciples came unto him; and he opened his mouth and taught them, saying:

"Blessed are the poor in spirit, for theirs is the kingdom of heaven. Blessed are they that mourn, for they shall be comforted. Blessed are the meek, for they shall inherit the earth. Blessed are they which do hunger and thirst after righteousness, for they shall be filled. Blessed are the merciful, for they shall obtain mercy. Blessed are the pure in heart, for they shall see God. Blessed are the peacemakers, for they shall be called the children of God. Blessed are they which are persecuted for righteousness' sake, for theirs is the kingdom of heaven.

"Blessed are ye, when men shall revile you, and persecute you, and shall say all manner of evil against you falsely, for my sake. Rejoice, and be exceeding glad, for great is your reward in heaven, for so persecuted they the prophets which were before you."

An extract from Matthew, 5: 1–12.

JESUS' TEACHING

If this was what the first Christians saw in Christ (as he came to be called, from the Greek word meaning "the anointed one") there were also in his teaching other elements susceptible of far wider application. The reported devotional ideas of Jesus do not go beyond the Jewish observances; service in the Temple, together with private prayer, were all that he indicated. In this very real sense, he lived and died a Jew. His moral teaching, though, focused upon repentance and deliverance from sin, and upon a deliverance available to all, and not just to Jews. Retribution had its part in Jesus' teaching (on this the Pharisees agreed with him), and, strikingly,

This tomb was dug into a rocky wall in the Kidron valley in the 1st century BCE. The body of Christ may have been placed in a similar tomb.

most of the more terrifying things said in the New Testament are attributed to him. Fulfilment of the Law was essential. Yet it was not enough; beyond observance lay the duties of repentance and restitution in the case of wrong done, even self-sacrifice. The law of love was the proper guide to action. Emphatically, Jesus rejected the role of the political leader. A political quietism was one of the meanings later discerned in a dictum which was to prove to be of terrible ambiguity: "My kingdom is not of this world."

Yet a Messiah who would be a political leader was expected by many. Others sought a leader against the Jewish religious establishment and therefore were potentially a danger to order even if they aimed only at religious purification and reform. Inevitably, Jesus, of the house of David, became a dangerous man

in the eyes of the authorities. One of his disciples was Simon the Zealot, an alarming associate because he had been a member of an extremist sect. Many of Jesus' teachings encouraged feeling against the dominant Sadducees and Pharisees, and they in their turn strove to draw out any anti-Roman implication which could be discerned in what he said.

THE FOLLOWERS OF CHRIST

POLITICAL FACTS PROVIDE the background to Jesus' destruction and the disappointment of the people; they do not explain the survival of his teaching. He had appealed not only to the politically dissatisfied but to Jews who felt that the Law was no longer guide

This 4th-century CE Christian sarcophagus is decorated with scenes from the Old and New Testaments, including, in the middle of the lower register, Christ's triumphal entry into Jerusalem.

The figure of Christ surrounded by the Apostles is depicted on a marble bas-relief from a 4th-century CE sarcophagus (subsequently used in the pulpit of the church of St Ambrose in Milan). The image of Christ, beardless and dressed as a Roman, is typical of early Christian art.

enough and to non-Jews who, though they might win second-class citizenship of Israel as proselytes, wanted something more to assure them of acceptance at the Last Day. Jesus had also attracted the poor and outcast; they were many in a society which offered enormous contrasts of wealth and no mercy to those who fell by the wayside. These were some of the appeals and ideas which were to yield in the end an astonishing harvest. Yet though they were effective in his own lifetime, they seemed to die with him. At his death his followers were only one tiny Jewish sect among many. But they believed that a unique thing had happened. They believed that Christ had risen from the dead, that they had seen him, and that he offered to them and those that were saved by his baptism the same overcoming of death and personal life after God's judgment. The generalization of this message and its presentation to the civilized world was achieved within a half-century of Jesus' death.

The conviction of the disciples led them to remain at Jerusalem, an important centre of pilgrimage for Jews from all over the Near East, and therefore a seminal centre for a new doctrine. Two of Jesus' disciples, Peter and Jesus' brother, James, were the leaders of the tiny group which awaited the imminent return of the Messiah, striving to prepare for it by penitence and the service of God in the Temple. They stood emphatically within the

Jewish fold; only the rite of baptism, probably, distinguished them. Yet other Jews saw in them a danger; their contacts with Greek-speaking Jews from outside Judaea led to questioning of the authority of the priests. The first martyr, Stephen, one of this group, was lynched by a Jewish crowd. One of those who witnessed this was a Pharisee from Tarsus of the tribe of Benjamin, named Paul. It may have been that as a Hellenized Jew of the dispersion he was especially conscious of the need for orthodoxy. He was proud of his own. Yet he is the greatest influence in the making of Christianity after Jesus himself.

Christ is depicted handing the keys of the Christian Church to St Peter in this 5th or 6th century CE mosaic from the church of Santa Costanza in Rome.

Dating from the 4th century CE, this mural from the catacomb of Domitilla in Rome shows Christ among the Apostles.

St Paul, depicted in this mosaic from the crypt of St Peter's in Rome, is thought to have been preaching during the 1st century CE. Through Paul's teaching, Christianity began to move away from its original Jewish roots and take on its own identity.

THE TEACHINGS OF ST PAUL

Somehow, Paul underwent a change of heart. From being a persecutor of the followers of Christ, he became one himself: it seems to have followed a sojourn of meditation and reflexion in the deserts of eastern Palestine. Then, in 47 CE (or perhaps earlier; dating

Paul's life and travels is a very uncertain business), he began a series of missionary journeys which took him all over the eastern Mediterranean. In 49 CE an apostolic council at Jerusalem took the momentous decision to send him as a missionary to gentiles, who would not be required to undergo the circumcision which was the most important act of submission to the Jewish faith; it is not clear whether he, the council, or both in agreement were responsible. There were already little communities of Jews following the new teaching in Asia Minor, where it had been carried by pilgrims. Now these were given a great consolidation by Paul's efforts. His especial targets were Jewish proselytes, gentiles to whom he could preach in Greek and who were now offered full membership of Israel through the new covenant. The doctrine that Paul taught was new. He rejected the Law (as Jesus had never done), and strove to reconcile the essentially Jewish ideas at the heart of Jesus' teaching with the conceptual world of the Greek language. He continued to emphasize the imminence of the coming end of things, but offered all nations, through Christ, the chance of understanding the mysteries of creation and, above all, of the relationship of things seen and things invisible, of the spirit and the flesh, and of the overcoming of the second by the first. In the process, Jesus became more than a human deliverer who had overcome death, and was God Himself – and this was to shatter the mould of Jewish thought within which the faith had been born. There was no lasting place for such an idea within Jewry, and Christianity was now forced out of the Temple. The intellectual world of Greece was the first of many new resting-places it was to find over the centuries. A colossal theoretical structure was to be built on this change.

The Acts of the Apostles give plentiful evidence of the uproar which such teaching

Paul writes to the Christians at Corinth

"For I delivered unto you first of all that which I also received, how that Christ died for our sins according to the scriptures; And that he was buried, and that he rose again the third day according to the scriptures: And that he was seen of Cephas, then of the twelve: After that, he was seen of above five hundred brethren at once; of whom the greater part remain unto this present, but some are fallen asleep. After that he was seen of James; then of all the Apostles. And last of all he was seen of me also, as of one born out of due time. For I am the least of the Apostles, that am not meet to be called an Apostle, because I persecuted the church of God. But by the grace of God I am what I am: And his grace which was bestowed upon me was not in vain; But I laboured more abundantly than they all: Yet not I, but the grace of God that was with me. Therefore whether it were I or they, so we preach, and so ye believed.

"Now if Christ be preached that he rose from the dead, how say some among you that there is no resurrection of the dead? But if there be no resurrection of the dead, then is Christ not risen: And if Christ be not risen, then is our preaching vain, and your faith is also vain."

An extract from 1 Corinthians, 15: 3–14.

could cause and also of the intellectually tolerant attitude of the Roman administration when public order was not involved. But it often was. In 59 CE, Paul had to be rescued from the Jews at Jerusalem by the Romans. When put on trial in the following year, he appealed to the emperor and to Rome he went, apparently with success. From that time he is lost to history; he may have perished in a persecution by Nero in 67 CE.

THE SPREAD OF CHRISTIANITY

The first age of Christian missions permeated the civilized world by sinking roots everywhere

St Paul's journeys

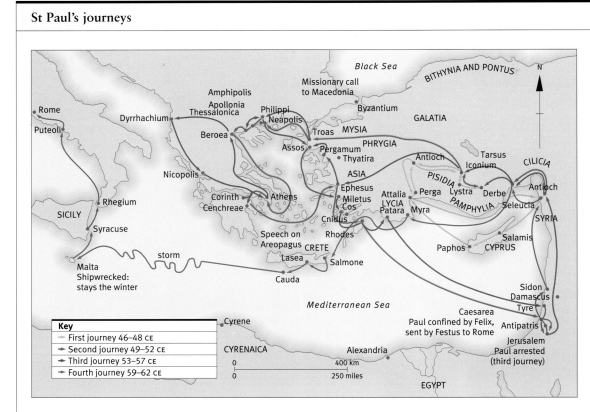

Key
→ First journey 46–48 CE
→ Second journey 49–52 CE
→ Third journey 53–57 CE
→ Fourth journey 59–62 CE

This map shows the routes St Paul is believed to have followed on his journeys, as described in the Acts of the Apostles. It appears that he visited numerous cities in the eastern Mediterranean, where he preached to Jews and non-Jews, with the aim of converting them to Christianity. St Paul taught that the Church should partly renounce its Jewish roots in order to allow gentiles also to hear the word and become Christians.

Through personal visits and long didactic letters, St Paul also spread his concept of the Church among the Christian communities that were already established in the region.

in the first place in the Jewish communities. The "Churches" which emerged were administratively independent of one another, though the community at Jerusalem was recognized to have an understandable primacy. There were to be found those who had seen the risen Christ and their successors. The only links of the Churches other than their faith were the institutional one of baptism, the sign of acceptance in the new Israel, and the ritual practice of the eucharist, the re-enactment of the rites performed by Jesus at his last supper with his disciples, the evening before his arrest. It has remained the central sacrament of the Christian Churches to this day.

The local leaders of the Churches exercised independent authority in practice, therefore, but this did not cover much. There was nothing except the conduct of the affairs of the local Christian community to be decided upon, after all. Meanwhile,

Christians waited for the Second Coming. Such influence as Jerusalem had flagged after 70 CE, when a Roman sack of the city dispersed many of the Christians there; after this time Christianity had less vigour within Judaea. By the beginning of the second century the communities outside Palestine were clearly more numerous and more important and had already evolved a hierarchy of officers to regulate their affairs. These identified the three later orders of the Church: bishops, presbyters and deacons. Their sacerdotal functions were at this stage minimal, and it was their administrative and governmental role which mattered.

JEWISH EXTREMISTS REBEL

The response of the Roman authorities to the rise of a new sect was largely predictable; its

THE DISPERSION

governing principle was that unless specific cause for interference existed, new cults were tolerated unless they awoke disrespect or disobedience to the empire. There was a danger at first that the Christians might be confounded with other Jews in a vigorous Roman reaction to Jewish nationalist movements which culminated in a number of bloody encounters, but their own political quietism and the announced hostility of other Jews saved them. Galilee itself had been in rebellion in 6 CE (perhaps a memory of it influenced Pilate's handling of the case of a Galilean among whose disciples was a Zealot) but a real distinction from Jewish nationalism came with the great Jewish rising of 66 CE. This was the most important in the whole history of Jewry under the empire, when the extremists gained the upper hand in Judaea and took over Jerusalem. The Jewish historian Josephus has recorded the atrocious struggle which followed, the final storming of the Temple, the headquarters of resistance, and its burning after the Roman victory. Before this, the unhappy inhabitants had been reduced to cannibalism in their struggle to survive. Archaeology has recently revealed at Masada, a little way from the city, what may well have been the site of the last stand of the Jews before it, too, fell to the Romans in 73 CE.

The Roman crushing of the rebellion was not the end of Jewish turbulence, but it was a turning-point. The extremists never again enjoyed such support and must have been discredited. The Law was now more than ever the focus of Jewishness, for the Jewish scholars and teachers (after this time, they are more and more designated as "rabbis") had continued to unfold its meaning in centres

This detail is from a 6th-century CE Roman sarcophagus decorated with scenes from the Passion. A symbolic representation of the Resurrection appears in the centre: a cross, upon which a monogram of Christ is held up by two doves. At the base of the cross are two Roman soldiers.

One of the most impressive examples of early Christian art, this mural from the catacomb of Priscilla in Rome dates from the middle of the 3rd century CE. The praying figure represents the deceased.

Jonah is depicted being thrown from a ship and about to be swallowed by the whale in this bas-relief on a 3rd-century CE sarcophagus. The biblical story of Jonah, who spent three days in the belly of the whale and emerged safe and sound, can be seen as an allegory of the resurrection that Christ promised his followers.

other than Jerusalem while the revolt was in progress. Their good conduct may have saved these Jews of the dispersion. Later disturbances were never so important as had been the great revolt, though in 117 CE Jewish riots in Cyrenaica developed into full-scale fighting, and in 132 CE the last "Messiah", Simon Bar Kochba, launched another revolt in Judaea. But the Jews emerged with their special status at law still intact. Jerusalem had been taken from them (Hadrian made it an Italian colony, which Jews might enter only once a year), but their religion was granted the privilege of having a special officer, a patriarch, with sovereignty over it, and they were allowed exemption from the obligations of Roman law which might conflict with their religious duties. This was the end of a volume of Jewish history. For the next eighteen hundred years Jewish history was to be the story of communities of the diaspora (dispersion), until a national state was again established in Palestine among the debris of another empire.

HOSTILITY TO CHRISTIANITY

THE NATIONALISTS of Judaea apart, Jews elsewhere in the empire were for a long time thereafter safe enough during the troubled years. Christians did less well, though their religion was not much distinguished from Judaism by the authorities; it was, after all, only a variant of Jewish monotheism with, presumably, the same claims to make. It was the Jews, not the Romans, who first persecuted it, as the Crucifixion itself, the martyrdom of Stephen and the adventures of Paul had shown. It was a Jewish king, Herod Agrippa, who, according to the author of the Acts of the Apostles, first persecuted the community at Jerusalem. It has even appeared plausible to some scholars that Nero, seeking a scapegoat for a great fire at Rome in 64 CE, should have had the Christians pointed out to him by hostile Jews. Whatever the source of this persecution, in which, according to popular Christian tradition, St Peter and St Paul both perished, and which was accompanied by horrific and bloody scenes in the arena, it seems to have been for a long time the end of any official attention by Rome to the Christians. They did not take up arms against the Romans in the Jewish revolts, and this must have soothed official suscepti-bilities with regard to them.

When they emerge in the administrative records as worth notice by government it is in the early second century CE. This is because of the overt dis-respect which Christians were by then showing in refusing to sacrifice to the emperor and the Roman deities. This was their distinction. Jews had a right to refuse; they had possessed a historic cult which the Romans respected – as they always respected such cults – when they took Judah under their rule. The Christians were now clearly seen as distinct from other Jews and were a recent creation. Yet the Roman attitude was that although

Nero (54–68 CE) was the first Roman emperor to persecute the Christians.

Christianity was not legal it should not be the subject of general persecution. If, on the other hand, breaches of the law were alleged – and the refusal to sacrifice might be one – then the authorities should punish when the allega-tions were specific and shown in court to be well founded. This led to many martyrdoms, as Christians refused the well-intentioned attempts of Roman civil ser-vants to persuade them to sacrifice or abjure their god, but there was no systematic attempt to eradicate the sect.

PERSECUTION

The authorities' hostility was, indeed, much less dangerous than that of the Christians' fellow-subjects. As the second century passed, there is more evidence of pogroms and poplar attacks on Christians, who were not pro-tected by the authorities since they followed

The Christian message

The Christian religion grew out of the preaching of Jesus of Nazareth, known as Christ, who transformed the monotheist tradition, exclusive to the Jewish people, into a message aimed at all of humankind regardless of social or ethnic differences. Some time after his death, various accounts of Christ's life and teachings were collected in the Gospels, which are included in the New Testament. Together with the earlier biblical writings (the Hebrew Bible, or Old Testament), this came to form the Christian Bible. For Christians, Christ represents the Son, the Father and the Holy Spirit which, combined, are the one and only God.

Christ's first followers were all Jews, like himself, but Christianity soon spread among other peoples, par-ticularly through the work of Paul of Tarsus, for whom Jesus' death was the redeeming act that atoned for the sins of the whole of humanity and with which he surpassed the Law of Moses. Christ's resurrection was seen as an example of the eternal life that could be attained by all those who obeyed the law of God, the law of justice and love.

Christian communities grew up all over the Roman Empire, their cohesion assured by a hierarchical system headed by the bishops. Christianity is currently the most widespread religion in the world.

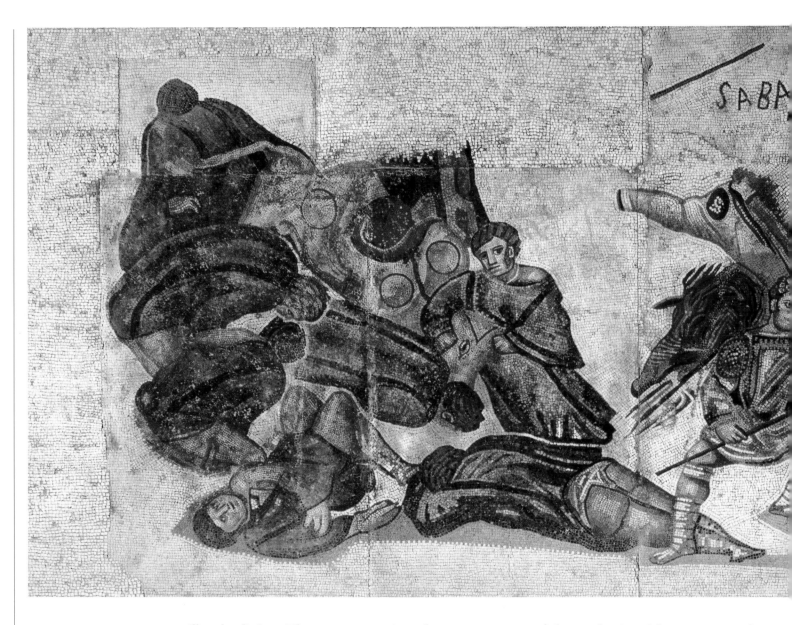

This Roman mosaic represents a spectacle, held in the amphitheatre, in which people were set on and killed by wild animals. Early Christians who refused to renounce their faith were often condemned to this terrible fate.

an illegal religion. They may sometimes have been acceptable scape-goats for the administration or lightning-conductors diverting dangerous currents. It was easy for the popular mind of a superstitious age to attribute to Christians the offences to the gods which led to famine, flood, plague and other natural disasters. Other equally convincing explanations of these things were lacking in a world with no other technique of explaining natural disaster. Christians were alleged to practise black magic, incest, even cannibalism (an idea no doubt explicable in terms of misleading

accounts of the Eucharist). They met secretly at night. More specifically and acutely, though we cannot be sure of the scale of this, the Christians threatened by their control of their members the whole customary structure which regulated and defined the proper relations of parents and children, husbands and wives, masters and slaves. They proclaimed that in Christ there was neither bond nor free and that he had come to bring not peace but a sundering sword to families and friends. It is not hard, therefore, to understand the violent outbursts

in the big provincial towns, such as that at Smyrna in 165 CE, or Lyons in 177 CE. They were the popular aspect of an intensification of opposition to Christianity which had an intellectual counterpart in the first attacks on the new cult by pagan writers.

THE CHURCH'S SURVIVAL

Persecution was not the only danger facing the early Church. Possibly it was the least grave. A much more serious one was that it might develop into just another cult of the kind of which many examples could be seen in the Roman Empire and, in the end, be engulfed like them in the magical morass of ancient religion. All over the Near East could be found examples of the "mystery religions", whose core was the initiation of the believer into the occult knowledge of a devotion centred on a particular god (the Egyptian Isis was a popular one, the Persian Mithras another). Almost always believers were offered the chance to identify themselves with the divine being in a ceremony

The Eucharist could be misinterpreted as a cannibalistic rite by those who mistrusted the Christians. This 3rd-century CE mural showing a Eucharistic banquet is from the catacomb of Priscilla in Rome.

Rome's Colosseum was opened in 80 CE. Many Christian martyrs died in the savage events that were staged there.

which involved a simulated death and resurrection and thus overcame mortality. Such cults offered, through their impressive rituals, the peace and liberation from the temporal which many craved. They were very popular.

THE GNOSTICS

The real danger that Christianity might develop into just another "mystery religion" is shown by the importance in the

second century of the Gnostics. Their name derives from the Greek word *gnosis*, meaning "knowledge": the knowledge the Christian Gnostics claimed was a secret, esoteric tradition, not revealed to all Christians but only to a few (one version said only to the Apostles and the sect to which it had subsequently descended). Some of their ideas came from Zoroastrian, Hindu and Buddhist sources which stressed the conflict of matter and spirit in a way which distorted the Judaeo-Christian tradition; some came from astrology and even magic. There was always a temptation in such a dualism, the attribution of evil and good to opposing principles and entities and the denial of the goodness of the material creation. The Gnostics were haters of this world and in some of their systems this led to the pessimism typical of the mystery cults; salvation was only possible by the acquisition of arcane knowledge, secrets of an initiated elect. A few Gnostics even saw Christ not as the saviour who confirmed and renewed a covenant but as one who delivered humanity from Yahweh's error. It was a dangerous creed in whatever form it came, for it cut at the roots of hopefulness which was the heart of the Christian revelation. It turned its back on the redemption of the here and now, of which Christians could never wholly despair, since they accepted the Judaic tradition that God made the world and that it was good.

In the second century, with its communities scattered throughout the diaspora and their organizational foundations fairly firmly settled, Christianity thus seems to stand at a parting of ways, either of which could prove fatal to it. Had it turned its back on the implications of Paul's work and remained merely a Jewish heresy, it would at best have been reabsorbed eventually into the Judaic tradition; on the other hand, a flight from a Jewry which rejected it might have

driven Christians into the Hellenistic world of the mystery cults or the despair of the Gnostics. Thanks to a handful of men, it escaped both.

THE FATHERS OF THE CHURCH

THE ACHIEVEMENT of the Fathers of the Church who navigated these perils was, for all its moral and pietistic content, above all intellectual. They were stimulated by their danger. Irenaeus, who succeeded the martyred Bishop of Lyons in 177 CE, provided the first

The Christians considered their doctrine to be the true philosophy, which explains the appearance of philosopher figures on several Christian sarcophagi. This marble relief from a 3rd-century CE sarcophagus shows a young Roman girl listening attentively to the teachings of a philosopher.

This mural painting is from the Teotecno family hypogeum (underground vault) in a 6th-century CE catacomb in Naples. Surrounded by lighted candles, members of the family are shown praying, waiting faithfully for the moment of resurrection. The scene presents a moving image of the peaceful approach to death that Christianity offers.

great outline of Christian doctrine, a creed and definition of the scriptural canon. All of these set off Christianity from Judaism. But he wrote also against the background of the challenge of heretical beliefs. In 172 CE the first Council had met to reject Gnostic doctrines. Christian doctrine was squeezed into intellectual respectability by the need to resist the pressures of competitors. Heresy and orthodoxy were born twins. One of the pilots who steered an emerging Christian theology through this period was the prodigiously learned Clement of Alexandria, a Christian Platonist (perhaps born in Athens), through whom Christians were brought to an understanding of what the Hellenistic tradition might mean apart from the mysteries. In particular, he directed Christians to the thought of Plato. To his even greater pupil, Origen, he transmitted the thought that God's truth was a reasonable truth, a belief which could attract those educated in the Stoic view of reality.

THE DIFFUSION OF CHRISTIANITY IN THE CLASSICAL WORLD

The intellectual drive of the early Fathers and the inherent social appeal of Christianity made it possible for it to utilize the huge possibilities of diffusion and expansion inherent in the structure of the classical and later Roman world. Its teachers could move freely and talk and write to one another in Greek. It had the great advantage of emerging in a religious age; the monstrous credulousness of the second century cloaks deep longings. They hint that the classical world is already running out of vigour; the Greek capital needed replenishment and one place to look for it was in new religions. Philosophy had become a religious quest and rationalism or scepticism appealed only to an infinitesimally small

minority. Yet this promising setting was also a challenge to the Church; early Christianity has to be seen always in the context of thriving competitors. To be born in a religious age was a threat as well as an advantage. How successfully Christianity met the threat and seized its opportunity was to be seen in the crisis of the third century, when the classical world all but collapsed and survived only by colossal, and in the end mortal, concession.

Christianity was to spread far beyond its birthplace and far beyond Rome in the centuries following the deaths of the Fathers of the Church. This Christian manuscript is from the Irish MacDurnan Gospels. Dating from the 9th century CE, it depicts St Luke holding a crozier and a book.

4 THE WANING OF THE CLASSICAL WEST

AFTER 200 CE THERE ARE many signs that Romans were beginning to look back on the past in a new way. Men and women had always talked of golden ages in the past, indulging in a conventional, literary nostalgia. But the third century brought something new for many inhabitants of the Roman Empire – a sense of conscious decline.

An image of Christ from the St Ermite catacomb in Rome. The figure's gestures and expression are reminiscent of Byzantine painting, which was developed by artists in the Eastern Roman Empire.

CRISIS AND CHANGE

Historians have spoken of a "crisis", but its most obvious expressions were in fact surmounted. The changes Romans carried out or accepted by the year 300 CE gave a new lease of life to much of classical Mediterranean civilization. They may even have been decisive in ensuring that it would in the end transmit so much of itself to the future. Yet the changes themselves took a toll, for some of them were essentially destructive of the spirit of that civilization. Restorers are often unconscious imitators. Somewhere about the beginning of the fourth century we can sense that the balance has tipped against the Mediterranean heritage. It is easier to feel it than to see what was the crucial moment. The signs are a sudden multiplication of ominous innovations – the administrative structure of the empire is rebuilt on new principles, its ideology is transformed, the religion of a once-obscure Jewish sect becomes established orthodoxy, and physically, large tracts of territory are given up to settlers from outside, alien immigrants. A century later still, and the consequence of these changes is apparent in political and cultural disintegration.

THE LAST EMPERORS' ROLE

The ups and downs of imperial authority mattered a lot in this process of disintegration. Classical civilization had come by the end of the second century CE to be coterminous with the empire. It was dominated by the conception of *romanitas*, the Roman way of doing things. Because of this, the weaknesses of the structure of government were fundamental to what was going wrong. The imperial office had long since ceased to be held, as Augustus had carefully pretended, by the agent of the Senate and people; the reality was a despotic monarch, his rule tempered only by such practical considerations as the placating of the Praetorian Guard on which he depended. A round of civil wars which followed the accession of the last, inadequate, Antonine emperor in 180 opened a terrible era. This wretched man, Commodus, was strangled by a wrestler at the bidding of his concubine and chamberlain in 192, but it solved nothing. From the struggles of four "emperors" in the months following his death there finally emerged an African, Septimius Severus, married to a Syrian, who strove to base the empire again on heredity, attempting to link his own family with the Antonine succession and thus to deal with one fundamental constitutional weakness.

THE IMPORTANCE OF THE ARMY

The emphasis Severus placed on hereditary succession was really to deny the fact of his own success. Like his rivals, he had been the candidate of a provincial army. Soldiers were the real emperor-makers throughout the third century and their power lay at the root of the empire's tendency to fragment. Yet the

Time chart (212 CE–476 CE)					
	212 CE Roman citizenship is granted to all free inhabitants of the empire	**325 CE** Council of Nicaea (first ecumenical council): condemnation of Arianism	**391 CE** Theodosius campaigns to Christianize the Roman Empire	**406 CE** Vandals cross the Roman border on the Rhine	**476 CE** Last Western Roman emperor is deposed
200 CE 250 CE 300 CE 350 CE 400 CE 450 CE 500 CE					
		313 CE Edict of Milan: tolerance of Christianity within the Roman Empire	**395 CE** Roman Empire is divided between East and West	**419 CE** Establishment of the Visigoth kingdom of Toulouse	

oman emperors wanted to be perceived as having the characteristics of heroes and of gods. This statue of Commodus portrays him in the guise of Hercules, with whom the 2nd-century CE emperor wished to be identified in order to magnify his authority.

soldiers could not be dispensed with; indeed, because of the barbarian threat, now present on several frontiers simultaneously, the army had to be enlarged and pampered. Here was a dilemma to face emperors for the next century. Severus' son Caracalla, who prudently began his reign by bribing the soldiers heavily, was none the less murdered by them in the end.

In theory the Senate still appointed the emperor. In fact it had little effective power except in so far as it could commit its prestige to one of a number of contending candidates. This was not much of an asset but still had some importance so long as the moral effect of maintaining the old forms was still significant. It was inevitable, though, that the arrangements should intensify the latent antagonism of Senate and emperor. Severus gave more power to officers drawn from the equestrian class; Caracalla inferred that a purge of the Senate would help and took this further step towards autocratic rule. More military emperors followed him; soon there was for the first time one who did not come from the senatorial ranks, though he was from the *equites*. Worse was to follow. In 235 Maximinus, a huge ex-ranker from the Rhine legions, contested the prize with an octogenarian from Africa who had the backing of the African army and, eventually, of the Senate. Many emperors were murdered by

their troops; one died fighting his own commander-in-chief in battle (his conqueror subsequently being slain by the Goths after his betrayal to them by one of his other officers). It was a dreadful century; altogether, twenty-two emperors came and went during it and that number does not include mere pretenders (or such semi-emperors as Postumus, who for a while maintained himself in Gaul, thus pre-figuring a later division of the empire).

During the 1st and 2nd centuries CE, under the emperors Septimius Severus and Caracalla, a new Roman theatre and forum were built in Lepcis Magna in the province of Africa.

ECONOMIC WEAKNESS

Though Severus' reforms had for a time improved matters, the fragility of his successors' position accelerated a decline in administration. Caracalla was the last emperor to try to broaden the basis of taxation by making all free inhabitants of the empire Roman citizens and thus liable to inheritance taxes, but no fundamental fiscal reform was attempted. Perhaps decline was inevitable, given the emergencies to be faced and the resources available. With irregularity and extemporization went growing rapacity and corruption as those with power or office used it to protect themselves. This reflected another problem, the economic

weakness which the empire was showing in the third century.

Few generalizations are safe about what this meant to the consumer and supplier. For all its elaboration and organization around a network of cities, the economic life of the empire was overwhelmingly agrarian. Its bedrock was the rural estate, the *villa*, large or small, which was the basic unit both of production and also, in many places, of society. Such estates were the source of subsistence for all those lived on them (and that meant nearly all the rural population). Probably, therefore, most people in the countryside were less affected by the long-term swings of the economy than by the requisitioning and heavier taxation which resulted from the

The Boscoreale Roman villa, a luxurious residence on the outskirts of Pompeii, was covered in lava when Mount Vesuvius erupted in 79 CE. This mural, which depicts an urban landscape framed by a pedestal and marble columns, was found in one of the villa's rooms.

This detail is from a fresco found in the Boscoreale villa. It dates from the mid-1st century BCE, when Hellenistic-style art was very fashionable. This scene may be an attempt to recreate the atmosphere of the Macedonian court.

empire ceasing to expand; the armies had to be supported from a narrower base. Sometimes, too, the land was devastated by fighting. But peasants lived at subsistence level, had always been poor, and continued to be so, whether bond or free. As times got worse, some sought to bind themselves as serfs, which suggests an economy in which money was in retreat before payment in goods and services. It also probably reflects

another impact of troubled times such as drove peasants to the towns or to banditry; the population everywhere sought protection.

Requisitioning and higher taxation may in some places have helped to produce depopulation – though the fourth century provides more evidence of this than the third – and to this extent were self-defeating. In any case, they were likely to be inequitable, for many of the rich were exempt from taxation and the

owners of the estates cannot have suffered much in inflationary times unless they were imprudent. The continuity of many of the great estate-owning families in antiquity does not suggest that the troubles of the third century bit deeply into their resources.

One of the signs of crisis within the 3rd-century CE empire was inflation – the value of money decreased while the price of goods on the market rose. Soldiers, and others who lived on fixed wages, were hard hit.

INFLATION AND INCREASING TAXATION

The administration and the army felt most of the effects of economic troubles, and particularly the major ill of the century, inflation. Its sources and extent are complex and still disputed. In part it derived from an official debasement of the coinage which was aggravated by the need to pay tribute in bullion to barbarians who from time to time were best placated by this means. But barbarian incursions themselves often helped to disrupt supply, and this again told against the cities, where prices rose. Because the soldiers' pay was fixed it fell in real value (this made them, of course, more susceptible to generals who offered lavish bribes). Although the overall impact is hard to assess, it has been suggested that money may have fallen during the century to about one-fiftieth of its value at the beginning.

The damage showed both in the towns and in imperial fiscal practice. From the third century onwards many towns shrank in size and prosperity; their early medieval successors were only pale reflexions of the important places they once had been. One cause was the increasing demands of the imperial tax-collectors. From the beginning of the fourth century the depreciation of coin led imperial officials to levy taxes in kind – they could often be used directly to supply local garrisons but were also the means of payment to civil servants – and this not only made the government more unpopular, but also the *curiales* or municipal office-holders who had the task of raising these impositions. By 300 they often had to be forced to take office, a sure sign that a once sought-after dignity had become a strenuous obligation. Some towns suffered from actual physical damage, too, especially those in the frontier regions. Significantly, as the third century wore on, towns well within the frontier began to rebuild (or build for the first time) walls for their protection. Rome began again to fortify itself soon after 270.

CONFRONTATION WITH PARTHIA

The army steadily grew bigger. If the barbarians were to be kept out it had to be paid, fed and equipped. If the barbarians were not kept out there would be tribute to pay to them instead. And there was not only the barbarian to contend with. Only in Africa was the imperial frontier reasonably secure against Rome's neighbours (because there

Rome's city walls were begun c.271 CE, at the time of the emperor Aurelian. The brick walls, intended to protect the city from Germanic incursions, incorporated defence towers and 14 main gates, which were later modified.

Palmyra, in present-day Syria, was an independent oasis city that lay between the Roman and Parthian empires. As a major caravan town, Palmyra enjoyed great wealth, of which its monumental buildings, now ruined, are the evidence.

were no neighbours there who mattered). In Asia things were much grimmer. Ever since the days of Sulla a cold war with Parthia had flared up from time to time into full-scale campaigning. Two things prevented the Romans and Parthians from ever really settling down peacefully. One was the overlapping of their spheres of interest. This was most obvious in Armenia, a kingdom which was alternately a buffer and shuttlecock between them for a century and a half, but the Parthians also dabbled in the disturbed waters of Jewish unrest, another sensitive matter for Rome. The other factor making for disturbance was the temptation presented to Rome time and time again by Parthia's own internal dynastic troubles.

Such facts had led in the second century CE to intense fighting over Armenia, its details often obscure. Severus eventually penetrated Mesopotamia but had to withdraw; the Mesopotamian valleys were too far away. The Romans were trying to do

too much and faced the classic problem of over-extended imperialism. But their opponents were tiring and at low ebb, too. Parthian written records are fragmentary, but the tale of exhaustion and growing incompetence emerges from a coinage declining into unintelligibility and blurred derivations from earlier Hellenized designs.

THE PERSIAN THREAT

In the third century Parthia disappeared, but the threat to Rome from the East did not. A turning-point was reached in the history of the old area of Persian civilization. In about 225 a king called Ardashir (later known in the West as Artaxerxes) killed the last king of Parthia and was crowned in Ctesiphon. He was to re-create the Achaemenid Empire of Persia under a new dynasty, the Sassanids; it would be Rome's greatest antagonist for more than four hundred years. There was much continuity here; the Sassanid Empire was Zoroastrian, as Parthia had been, and evoked the Achaemenid tradition as Parthia had done.

Within a few years the Persians had invaded Syria and opened three centuries of struggle with the empire. In the third century there was not a decade without war. The Persians conquered Armenia and took one emperor (Valerian) prisoner. Then they were driven from Armenia and Mesopotamia in 297. This gave the Romans a frontier on the Tigris, but it was not one they could keep for ever. Neither could the Persians keep their conquests. The outcome was a long-drawn-out and ding-dong contest. A sort of equilibrium grew up in the fourth and fifth centuries and only in the sixth did it begin to break down. Meanwhile, commercial ties appeared. Though trade at the frontier was officially limited to three designated towns, important colonies of Persian merchants came to live in the great cities of the empire. Persia, moreover, lay across trade routes to India and China which were as vital to Roman exporters as to those who wanted

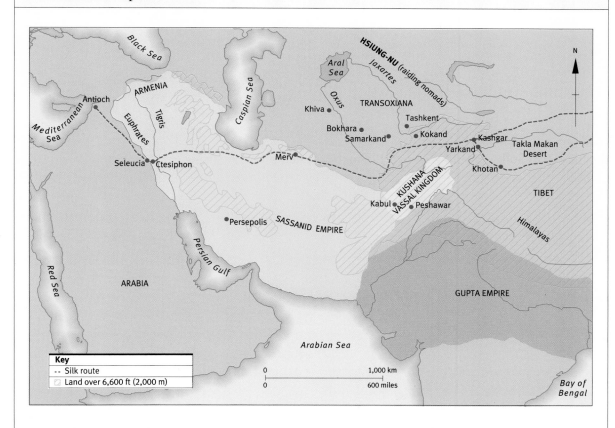

The Sassanid Empire c.400 CE

Key
- - Silk route
- Land over 6,600 ft (2,000 m)

Around 225 CE, Ardashir, conqueror of the last Parthian king, re-created the ancient Persian kingdom under the new Sassanid Dynasty. The Persians quickly launched an invasion of Syria and attempted to increase their hold on the Near East. Many of the main commercial trading routes to the India and the Far East crossed Persian territory, including the famous Silk Route that made it possible for the Roman Empire to import valuable goods such as spices, gems and silk from China. From the late 3rd century CE, the Romans and the Persians began to hold negotiations concerning the silk trade.

The arch built in 203 CE in honour of Septimius Severus and his children dominates the western end of the Roman Forum. It is decorated with bas-reliefs portraying the emperor's military campaigns against the Parthians and the Arabs.

oriental silk, cotton and spices. Yet these ties did not offset other forces. When not at war, the two empires tended to co-exist with cold hostility; their relations were complicated by communities and peoples settled on both sides of the frontier, and there was always the danger of the strategic balance being upset by a change in one of the buffer kingdoms – Armenia, for instance. The final round of open struggle was long put off, but came at last in the sixth century.

This is to jump too far ahead for the present; by then huge changes had taken place in the Roman Empire which have still to be explained. The conscious dynamism of the Sassanid monarchy was only one of the pressures encouraging them. Another came from the barbarians along the Danube and Rhine frontiers. The origins of the folk-movements which propelled them forward in the third century and thereafter must be sought in a long development and are less important than the outcome. These peoples grew more insistent, acted in larger groupings and had, in the end, to be allowed to settle inside Roman territory. Here they were first engaged as soldiers to protect the empire against other barbarians and then, gradually, began to take a hand in running the empire themselves.

A Roman military camp

This plan of a Roman encampment is based on descriptions of such camps given in a military treatise drawn up between the 1st and 3rd centuries CE. A typical Roman army camp was designed to accommodate 40,000 men. The complex was surrounded by a wall of earth, peat or stone and had a moat. Inside, two main roads running parallel across the minor axis of the camp divided the space into three principal sections.

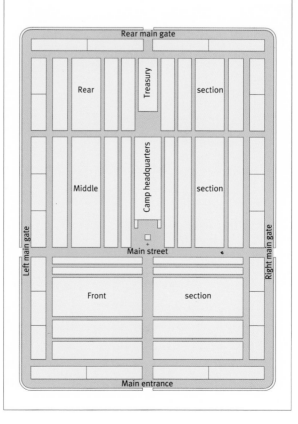

THE EUROPEAN THREAT

In 200 the assimilation of barbarians into the empire still lay in the future; all that was clear then was that new pressures were building up. The most important barbarian peoples involved were the Franks and Alamanni on the Rhine and the Goths on the lower Danube. From about 230 the empire was struggling to hold them off but the cost of fighting on two fronts was heavy; his Persian entanglements soon led one emperor to make concessions to the Alamanni. When his immediate successors added their own quarrels to their Persian burdens, the Goths took advantage of a promising situation and invaded Moesia, the province immediately south of the Danube, killing an emperor there *en passant* in 251. Five years later, the Franks crossed the Rhine. The Alamanni followed and got as far as Milan. Gothic armies invaded Greece and raided Asia and the Aegean from the sea. Within a few years the European dams seemed to give way everywhere at once.

The scale of these incursions is not easy to establish. Perhaps the barbarians could never field an army of more than twenty or thirty thousand. But this was too much at any one

This scene is from a Sassanid rock relief in the Naqsh-i-Rustam pass, north of Persepolis. It represents the mounted forces of King Ardashir, following his victory over the last Parthian king c.225. Ardashir, on the left, is depicted receiving a diadem from the god Mazda. Defeated Parthians lie trampled beneath the horses' hooves.

Daily life in Roman cities

From the 3rd century BCE, more and more Romans took to city life. As the cities expanded, artisanal and commercial activities within them became increasingly important. Numerous funeral monument decorations give us a good idea of the kind of trades that existed. Most businesses were on a small scale: the artisans' workshops were often family-run, perhaps employing a few slaves and apprentices, and also serving as a shop for the mainly local clientele. Tools were simple, except in the large-scale construction industry, where more complex machinery was occasionally used.

Many of the shops in and around the crowded markets sold foodstuffs, competing with pedlars. Some taverns offered ready-prepared food to travellers. Most city-dwellers spent a great deal of time in the streets and did not eat at fixed times.

Ordinary people cooked very little. In houses belonging to wealthy Romans, however, slaves often prepared lavish meals. Meat and fish dishes were rarely eaten without some kind of sauce. These sauces were based on aromatic herbs, pepper, pickles, oil, vinegar, wine and honey.

Trajan's Markets were constructed by the emperor Trajan on the western side of the Forum in the 2nd century CE. Paid for by the gains from the Dacian wars, this large vaulted structure housed shops and commercial properties. The six-storey complex was bounded by a semicircular public space, the exedra.

place for the imperial army. Its backbone was provided by recruits from the Illyrian provinces; appropriately, it was a succession of emperors of Illyrian stock who turned the tide. Much of what they did was simple good soldiering and intelligent extemporization.

They recognized priorities; the main dangers lay in Europe and had to be dealt with first. Alliance with Palmyra helped to buy time against Persia. Losses were cut; trans-Danubian Dacia was abandoned in 270. The army was reorganized to provide effective

mobile reserves in each of the main danger areas. This was all the work of Aurelian, whom the Senate significantly called "Restorer of the Roman Empire". But the cost was heavy. A more fundamental reconstruction was implicit if the work of the Illyrian emperors was to survive and this was the aim of Diocletian. A soldier of proven bravery, he sought to restore the Augustan tradition but revolutionized the empire instead.

THE AGE OF DIOCLETIAN

DIOCLETIAN HAD an administrator's genius rather than a soldier's. Without being especially imaginative, he had an excellent grasp of organization and principles, a love of order and great skill in picking and trusting men to whom he could delegate. He was also energetic. Diocletian's capital was wherever the imperial retinue found itself; it moved about the empire, passing a year here, a couple of months there, and sometimes only a day or two in the same place. The heart of the reforms which emerged from this court was a division of the empire intended to deliver it both from the dangers of internal quarrels between pretenders in remote provinces and

from the over-extension of its administrative and military resources. In 285 Diocletian appointed a co-emperor, Maximian, with responsibility for the empire west of a line running from the Danube to Dalmatia. The two *augusti* were subsequently each given a *caesar* as coadjutor; these were to be both their assistants and their successors, thus making possible an orderly transfer of power. In fact, the machine of succession only once operated as Diocletian intended, at his own abdication and that of his colleague, but the practical separation of administration in two imperial structures was not reversed. After this time all emperors had to accept a large measure of division even when there was nominally still only one of them.

There also now emerged explicitly a new conception of the imperial office. No longer was the title *princeps* employed; the emperors were the creation of the army, not the Senate, and were deferred to in terms recalling the semi-divine kingship of oriental courts. Practically, they acted through pyramidal bureaucracies. "Dioceses" responsible directly to the emperors through their "vicars" grouped provinces much smaller and about twice as numerous as the old ones had been. The senatorial monopoly of governmental power had long since gone; senatorial rank now meant in effect merely a social distinction (membership of the wealthy land-owning class) or occupation of one of the important bureaucratic posts. Equestrian rank disappeared.

THE TETRARCHY

The military establishment of the Tetrarchy, as it was called, was much larger (and, therefore, more expensive) than that laid down originally by Augustus. The theoretical mobility of the legions, deeply dug into long-occupied garrisons, was abandoned. The army of the frontiers was now broken up into units, some of which remained permanently in the same place while others provided new

Diocletian and Maximian were the two emperors who, together with their respective *caesars*, formed the first government within the tetrarchic system organized by Diocletian at the end of the 3rd century CE. This porphyry sculpture, which dates from c.300 CE, symbolizes the tetrarchs' solidarity.

mobile forces smaller than the old legions. Conscription was reintroduced. Something like a half-million men were under arms. Their direction was wholly separated from the civilian government of the provinces with which it had once been fused.

The results of this system do not seem to have been exactly what Diocletian envisaged. They included a considerable measure of military recovery and stablization, but its cost was enormous. An army whose size doubled in a century had to be paid for by a population which had probably grown smaller. Heavy taxation not only compromised the loyalty of the empire's subjects and encouraged corruption; it also required a close control of social arrangements so that the tax base should not be eroded. There was great administrative pressure against social mobility; the peasant, for example, was obliged to stay where he was recorded at the census. Another celebrated (though so far as can be seen totally unsuccessful) example was the attempt to regulate wages and prices throughout the empire by a freeze. Such efforts, like those to raise more taxation, meant a bigger civil service, and as the number of administrators increased so, of course, did the overheads of government.

THE IDEOLOGICAL CRISIS

In the end Diocletian probably achieved most by opening the way to a new view of the imperial office itself. The religious aura which it acquired was a response to a real problem. Somehow, under the strain of continued usurpation and failure the empire had ceased to be unquestioningly accepted. This was not merely because of dislike of higher taxation or fear of its growing numbers of secret police. Its ideological basis had been eroded and it could not focus loyalties. A crisis of civilization was going on as well as a crisis of government. The spiritual matrix of the classical world was breaking up; neither state nor civilization was any longer to be taken for granted and they needed a new ethos before they could be.

An emphasis on the unique status of the emperor and his sacral role was one early response to this need. Consciously, Diocletian acted as a saviour, a Jupiter-like figure holding back chaos. Something in this spoke of affinities with those thinkers of the late classical world who saw life as a perpetual struggle of good and evil. Yet this was a vision not Greek or Roman at all, but oriental. The acceptance of a new vision of the emperor's relation to the gods, and therefore of a new conception of the official cult, did not bode well for the traditional practical tolerance of the Greek world. Decisions about worship might now decide the fate of the empire.

THE GROWTH OF THE CHRISTIAN CHURCH

CHANGES IN THE ATTITUDES of successive Roman emperors were now to shape the history of the Christian Churches for both good and ill. In the end Christianity was to be the legatee of Rome. Many religious sects have risen from the position of persecuted minorities to become establishments in their own right. What sets the Christian Church apart is that this took place within the uniquely comprehensive structure of the late Roman Empire, so that it both attached itself to and strengthened the lifeline of classical civilization, with enormous consequences not only for itself but for Europe and ultimately the world.

At the beginning of the third century missionaries had already carried the faith to

the non-Jewish peoples of Asia Minor and North Africa. Particularly in North Africa, Christianity had its first mass successes in the towns; it long remained a predominantly urban phenomenon. But it was still a matter of minorities. Throughout the empire, the old gods and the local deities held the peasants' allegiance. By the year 300 Christians may have made up only about a tenth of the population of the empire. But there had already been striking signs of official favour and even concession. One emperor had been

The St Simeon basilica in Qalaat Semaan, Syria, was constructed c.480 CE. Its impressive remains, such as this section from the central octagon, testify to the robustness of Christian churches built in the Near East during the 4th and 5th centuries.

Paul of Tarsus was a Greek-speaking Roman citizen and a Pharisee from Cilicia. Following his conversion to Christianity, he became a key figure in the early Church, spreading his belief that Christianity was not a religion exclusive to the Jews.

nominally a Christian and another had included Jesus Christ among the gods honoured privately in his household. Such contacts with the court illustrate an interplay of Jewish and classical culture which is an important part of the story of the process by which Christianity took root in the empire. Perhaps Paul of Tarsus, the Jew who could talk to Athenians in terms they understood, had launched this. Later, early in the second century, Justin Martyr, a Palestinian Greek, had striven to show that Christianity had a debt to Greek philosophy. This had a political point; cultural identification with the classical tradition helped to rebut the charge of disloyalty to the empire. If a Christian could stand in the ideological heritage of the Hellenistic world he could also be a good citizen, and Justin's rational Christianity (even though he was martyred for it in about 165) envisaged a revelation of the Divine Reason in which all the great philosophers and prophets had partaken, Plato among them, but which was only complete in Christ. Others were to follow similar lines, notably the learned Clement of Alexandria, who strove to integrate pagan scholarship with Christianity, and Origen (though his exact teaching is still debated because of the disappearance of many of his writings). A North African Christian, Tertullian, had contemptuously asked what the Academy had to do with the Church; he was answered by the Fathers who deliberately employed the conceptual armoury of Greek philosophy to provide a statement of the Faith which anchored Christianity to rationality as Paul had not done.

THE PERSECUTION OF CHRISTIANS

When coupled to its promise of salvation after death and the fact that the Christian life could be lived in a purposeful and optimistic

This relief from a sarcophagus, probably of Christian origin, dates from the 2nd or 3rd century CE. A philosopher is depicted, book in hand, with a man and a woman. The classical and monumental style is reminiscent of compositions that were often used to decorate pagan sarcophagi.

way, such developments might lead us to suppose that Christians were by the third century confident about the future. In fact, favourable portents were much less striking than the persecutions so prominent in the history of the early Church. There were two great outbreaks. That of the middle of the century expressed the spiritual crisis of the establishment. It was not only economic strain and military defeat that were troubling the empire, but a dialectic inherent in Roman success itself: the cosmopolitanism which had been so much the mark of the empire was, inevitably, a solvent of the *romanitas* which was less and less a reality and more and more a slogan. The emperor Decius seems to have been convinced that the old recipe of a return to traditional Roman virtue and values could still work; it implied the revival of service to the gods whose benevolence would then be once more deployed in favour of the empire. The Christians, like others, must sacrifice to the Roman tradition, said Decius, and many did, to judge by the certificates

Constantine, Roman emperor in the years 306–337 CE, was, in the eyes of some, the "thirteenth Apostle", due to what he did for the Christian Church. His effigy appears on this gold coin.

issued to save them from persecution; some did not, and died. A few years later, Valerian renewed persecution on the same grounds, though his proconsuls addressed themselves rather to the directing personnel and the property of the Church – its buildings and books – than to the mass of believers. Thereafter, persecution ebbed, and the Church resumed its shadowy, tolerated existence just below the horizon of official attention.

Persecution had shown, nevertheless, that it would require great efforts and prolonged determination to eradicate the new sect; it may even have been already beyond the capacities of Roman government to carry out such an eradication. The exclusiveness and isolation of early Christianity had waned. Christians were increasingly prominent in local affairs in the Asian and African provinces. Bishops were often public figures with whom officials expected to do business; the development of distinct traditions within the Faith (those of the Churches of Rome, Alexandria and Carthage being the most important) spoke for the degree to which it was rooted in local society and could express local needs.

Outside the empire, too, there had been signs that better times might lie ahead for Christianity. The local rulers of the client states under the shadow of Persia could not afford to neglect any source of local support. Respect for widely held religious views was at least prudent. In Syria, Cilicia and Cappadocia, Christians had been very successful in their missionary work and in some towns they formed a social élite. Simple superstition, too, helped to convince kings; the Christian god might prove powerful and it could hardly be damaging to insure against his ill-will. Thus Christianity's political and civic prospects improved.

Christians noted with some satisfaction that their persecutors did not prosper; the Goths slew Decius, and Valerian was said to have been skinned alive by the Persians (and stuffed). But Diocletian did not appear to draw any conclusions from this and in 303 launched the last great Roman persecution. It was not at first harsh. The main targets were Christian officials, clergy and the books and buildings of the Church. The books were to be handed over for burning, but for some time there was no death penalty for failing to sacrifice. (Many Christians none the less did sacrifice, the bishop at Rome among them.) Constantius, the *caesar* of the West, did not enforce the persecution after 305 when Diocletian abdicated, though his Eastern colleague (Diocletian's successor Galerius) felt strongly about it, ordering a general sacrifice on pain of death. This meant that persecution was worst in Egypt and Asia where it was kept up a few years longer. But before this it had been cut across by the complicated politics which led to the emergence of the emperor Constantine the Great.

CONSTANTINE THE GREAT

THE FATHER OF Constantine the Great was Constantius, who died in Britain in 306, a year after his accession as *augustus*. Constantine was there at the time and although he had not been his father's *caesar* he was hailed as emperor by the army at York. A troubled period of nearly two decades followed. Its intricate struggles demonstrated the failure of Diocletian's arrangements for the peaceful transmission of the empire and only ended in 324, when Constantine reunited the empire under one ruler.

By this time he had already addressed himself vigorously and effectively to its

Constantinople

In 324 CE Constantine, having become sole emperor with his defeat of Licinius, decided to build a new imperial capital on the site of Byzantium in the Eastern Empire. On 11 May 330 CE, the "new Rome" – a Christian city from the outset – was inaugurated and a column of porphyry crowned with a statue of Constantine was erected at its centre. During the whole Byzantine era, this column was the symbol of the foundation and perpetuity of the capital.

It was only from the end of the 4th century that Constantinople became the definitive headquarters of the Eastern Empire – the city in which the emperor showed himself in public and asserted his divine and imperial power. During the Middle Ages, the city again assumed the name of Byzantium, which it retained until its conquest by the Turks in 1453 CE.

Constantinople's enviable strategic position between Europe and Asia, with control of the Bosphorus Straits, meant that it enjoyed rapid economic growth. A large number of artisans and tradespeople set up their businesses in the capital, where they were able to obtain materials and products from all over the East and export them to the Western Roman Empire.

The city's expansion was accompanied by a public building programme, during which churches, squares and municipal offices were constructed. In the 5th century, according to a contemporary survey, Constantinople had 14 churches, 11 imperial palaces, 5 markets, 8 public baths and 153 private ones, 20 public bakeries and 120 private ones, 322 streets and a total of 4,388 houses.

This French miniature of Constantinople by Péronet Lamy dates from 1436 CE and depicts the capital of the Eastern Roman Empire less than 20 years before its downfall.

problems, though with more success as a soldier than as an administrator. Often with barbarian recruits, he built up a powerful field army distinct from the frontier guards; it was stationed in cities within the empire. This was a strategically sound decision which proved itself in the fighting power the empire showed in the East for the next two centuries. Constantine also disbanded the Praetorian Guard and created a new, German bodyguard. He restored a stable gold currency and paved the way to the abolition of payments of taxes in kind and the restoration of a money economy. His fiscal reforms had more mixed results but attempted some readjustment of the weight of taxation so that more should be borne by the rich. None of these things, though, so struck contemporaries as his attitude to Christianity.

CONSTANTINE AND THE CHURCH

Constantine gave the Church official houseroom. He thus played a more important part in shaping its future than any other Christian layman and was to be called the "thirteenth Apostle". Yet his personal relationship to

Rome's mausoleum of St Constance, the interior of which is shown here, was built in the 4th century CE during the reign of Constantine. The domed central room is encircled by 12 pairs of twin columns with composite capitals supporting large arches. Originally, the sarcophagus of Constantina, the emperor's daughter, stood beneath one of these arches.

Christianity was complicated. He grew up intellectually with the monotheistic predisposition of many late classical men and women and was in the end undoubtedly a convinced believer (it was not then unusual for Christians to do as he did and postpone baptism until their deathbed). But he believed from fear and hope, for the god he worshipped was a god of power. His first adherence was to the sun-god whose sign he bore and whose cult was already officially associated with that of the emperor. Then, in 312, on the eve of battle and as a result of what he believed to be a vision he ordered his soldiers to put on their shields a Christian monogram. This showed a willingness to show suitable respect to whatever gods there might be. He won the battle and thenceforth, though continuing publicly to acknowledge the cult of the sun, he began to show important favours to the Christians and their god.

THE EDICT OF MILAN

One manifestation of the emperor's new enthusiasm for Christianity was an edict the following year which was issued by another of the contenders for the empire, after agreement with Constantine at Milan. It restored to Christians their property, and granted them the toleration that other religions enjoyed. The justification may reveal Constantine's own thinking as well as his wish to arrive at a satisfactory compromise formula with his colleague, for it explained its provisions by the hope "that whatever divinity dwells in the heavenly seat may be appeased and be propitious towards us and to all who are placed under our authority". Constantine went on to make considerable gifts of property to the churches, favouring, in particular, that of Rome. Besides providing important tax concessions to the clergy, he conferred an unlimited right to receive bequests on the Church. Yet for years his coins continued to honour pagan gods, notably the "Unconquered Sun".

CHURCH AND STATE

Constantine gradually came to see himself as having a quasi-sacerdotal role, and this was of the first importance in the further evolution of the imperial office. He saw himself as responsible to God for the well-being of the Church to which he more and more publicly and unequivocally adhered. After 320 the sun no longer appeared on his coins and soldiers had to attend church parades. But he was always cautious of the susceptibilities of his pagan subjects. Though he later despoiled temples of their gold while building splendid Christian churches and encouraging converts by preferment, he did not cease to tolerate the old cults.

In some of Constantine's work (like that of Diocletian) there was the development of things latent and implicit in the past, an extension of earlier precedents. This was true of his interventions in the internal affairs of the Church. As early as 272, the Christians of Antioch had appealed to the emperor to remove a bishop and Constantine himself in 316 tried to settle a controversy in North Africa by installing a bishop of Carthage against the will of a local sectarian group

The lack of individuality in this bronze bust of Constantine represents his divine authority. It marks the birth of a new style, emphasizing the superiority of emperors who saw themselves as guardians of the Church.

known as Donatists. Constantine came to believe that the emperor owed to God more than a grant of freedom to the Church or even an endowment. His conception of his role evolved towards that of the guarantor and, if need be, the imposer of the unity which God required as the price of His continuing favour. When he turned on the Donatists it was this view of his duty which gave them the unhappy distinction of being the first schismatics to be persecuted by a Christian government. Constantine was the creator of Caesaropapism, the belief that the secular ruler has divine authority to settle religious belief, and of the notion of established religion in Europe for the next thousand years.

Dura-Europos, built as a fortress by the Hellenistic Seleucid monarchy, was a Roman stronghold from 165 CE. The fortress incorporated elements from both Eastern and Western culture. Archaeological findings suggest that near the temples to the Roman gods there stood a synagogue, a sanctuary dedicated to Mithras and a Christian church.

This mosaic from the dome of the Arian Baptistry in Ravenna dates from c.500 CE. The baptism of Christ is depicted in the centre, with John the Baptist on the right and a personification of the river Jordan on the left. The scene is surrounded by the 12 Apostles and a throne, upon which a cross is raised.

THE COUNCIL OF NICAEA

Constantine's greatest act in the ordering of religion came just after he had formally declared himself a Christian in 324 (a declaration preceded by another victory over an imperial rival who had, interestingly, been persecuting Christians). This was the calling of the first ecumenical council, the Council of Nicaea. It met for the first time in 325, nearly

300 bishops being present, and Constantine presided over it. Its task was to settle the response of the Church to a new heresy, Arianism, whose founder, Arius, taught that the Son did not share the divinity of the Father. Though technical and theological, the nice issues to which this gave rise prompted enormous controversy. Grave scandal was alleged by Arius' opponents. Constantine sought to heal the division and the Council

laid down a Creed which decided against the Arians, but went on in a second reunion to re-admit Arius to communion after suitable declarations. That this did not satisfy all the bishops (and that there were few from the West at Nicaea) was less important than that Constantine had presided at this crucial juncture of proclaiming the emperor's enjoyment of special authority and responsibility. The Church was clothed in the imperial purple.

Constantine is shown being crowned by the hand of God on this 4th-century CE gold medal. The emperor's children are at his side, receiving crowns from Victoria.

unsettled when Arius died, and Constantine's own death followed not long after. Yet Arianism was not to prosper in the East. Its last successes, instead, were won by Arian missionaries to the Germanic tribes of southeast Russia; borne by these barbarian nations, Arianism was to survive until the seventh century in the West – but this is to anticipate.

CHRISTIANITY DIVIDED

There were other great implications, too. Behind the hair-splitting of the theologians lay a great question both of practice and of principle: in the new ideological unity given to the empire by the official establishment of Christianity, what was to be the place of diverging Christian traditions which were social and political, as well as liturgical and theological, realities? The churches of Syria and Egypt, for example, were strongly tinctured by their inheritance of thought and custom both from the Hellenistic culture and the popular religion of those regions. The importance of such considerations helps to explain why the practical outcome of Constantine's ecclesiastical policy was less than he had hoped. The Council did not produce an emollient formula to make easier a general reconciliation in a spirit of compromise. Constantine's own attitude to the Arians soon relaxed (in the end, it was to be an Arian bishop who baptized him as he lay dying) but the opponents of Arius, led by the formidable Athanasius, bishop of Alexandria, were relentless. The quarrel remained

CONSTANTINE'S LEGACY

How much of the Church's rise was in the end inevitable it is hardly profitable to consider. Certainly – in spite of a North African

Arius was a 3rd-century CE Christian priest from Alexandria. His teaching, which spread among the Germanic peoples, also reached Ravenna, where an Arian baptistry, shown below, still stands. In 325 Arianism was condemned as heresy at the Council of Nicaea, which was presided over by Constantine.

Scenes on the triumphal arch dedicated to the emperor Galerius in Thessalonica depict his 4th-century CE military campaigns. In this detail, Galerius is shown taking part in a triumphal procession.

These elaborate clasps were found in the tomb of a 5th-century CE Germanic princess. They were probably brought to the West from the Pontus region.

Christian tradition which saw the state as an irrelevancy – something so positively important as Christianity could hardly have remained for ever unrecognized by the civil power. Yet someone had to begin. Constantine was the man who took the crucial steps which linked Church and empire for so long as the empire should last. His choices were historically decisive. The Church gained most, for it acquired the charisma of Rome. The empire seemed less changed. Yet Constantine's sons were brought up as Christians and even if the fragility of much in the new establishment was to appear soon after his death in 337, he had registered a decisive break with the tradition of classical Rome. Ultimately, unwittingly, he founded Christian Europe and, therefore, the modern world.

One of his decisions only slightly less enduring in its effects was his foundation, "on the command of God", he said, of a city to rival Rome on the site of the old Greek colony of Byzantium at the entrance to the Black Sea. It was dedicated in 330 as Constantinople. Though his own court remained at Nicomedia and no emperor was to reside there permanently until another fifty years were past, Constantine was again shaping the future. For a thousand years Constantinople would be a Christian capital, unsullied by pagan rites. After that, for five hundred years more, it would be a pagan capital and the constant ambition of would-be successors to its traditions.

DISUNITY IN THE EMPIRE

The empire as Constantine left it was, in Roman eyes, still coterminous with civilization. Its frontiers ran for the most part along natural features which recognized, more or less, the demarcations of distinct geographical or

The two parts of the Roman Empire

After the 3rd century CE, the differences between the Eastern and Western Roman Empires became increasingly noticeable. There was a sharp fall in the populations of many Western cities around this time, accompanied by a decrease in trade and reduced rates of production. This decline contrasted sharply with the dynamism of the Eastern Mediterranean cities, which continued to reap the benefits of their commercial and diplomatic relationships with the Far East.

Moreover, the Eastern Empire's geographical position meant that most of the principal invasion routes did not cross her territories – the rampaging barbarian hordes tended to move westward from the vast plains of central Europe.

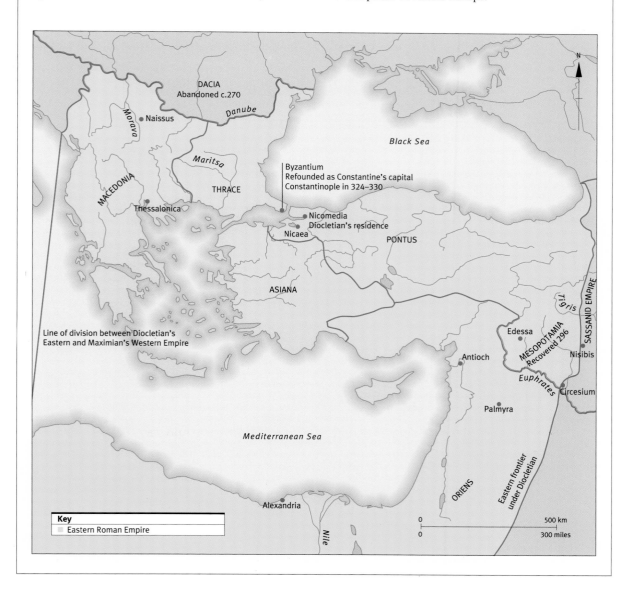

historical regions. Hadrian's Wall in Britannia was their northern limit; in continental Europe they followed the Rhine and Danube. The Black Sea coasts north of the mouths of the Danube had been lost to barbarians by 305 BCE, but Asia Minor remained in the empire; it stretched as far east as the shifting boundary with Persia. Further south, the Levant coast and Palestine lay within a frontier which ran to the Red Sea. The lower Nile valley was still held by the empire and so was the North African coast; the African frontiers were the Atlas and the desert.

This unity was, for all Constantine's great work, in large measure an illusion. As the first experiments with co-emperors had shown, the world of Roman civilization had grown too big for a unified political structure, however desirable the preservation of the myth of unity might be. Growing cultural differentiation between a Greek-speaking East and a Latin-speaking West, the new importance of Asia Minor, Syria and Egypt (in all of which there were large Christian communities) after the establishment of Christianity and the continuing stimulus of direct contact with Asia in the East all drove the point home. After 364 the two parts of the old empire were only once more and then only briefly ruled by the same man. Their institutions diverged further and further. In the East the emperor was a theological as well as a juridical figure; the identity of empire and Christendom and the emperor's standing as the expression of divine intention were unambiguous. The West, on the other hand, had by 400 already seen

The migration of the Germanic peoples

The great population movements that affected the Roman Empire during the 4th and 5th centuries CE transformed the cultural map of Europe and dealt the decadent Western Empire its death-blow. The barbarian invasions differed in their effects: some tribes were determined to occupy territories and property by force, others destroyed everything they found in their path, while others made an effort to settle more peacefully, looking for recognition from the Romans. The invaders were often not very numerous, but the local populations offered little or no resistance. As a result, several independent kingdoms emerged, such as the Visigothic kingdom in Hispania and the Frankish kingdom in Gaul, both former Roman provinces.

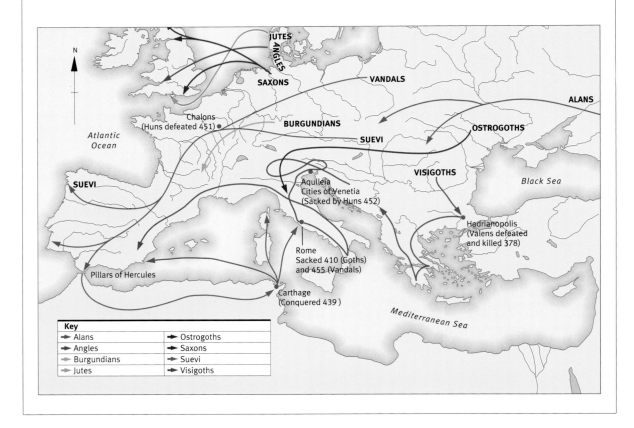

adumbrated the distinction of the roles of Church and State which was to father one of the most creative arguments of European politics. There was an economic contrast, too: the East was populous and could still raise great revenues, while the West was by 300 already unable to feed itself without Africa and the Mediterranean islands. It now seems obvious that two distinct civilizations were to emerge, but it was a long time before any of the participants could see that.

THE DECLINE OF THE WEST

In the event, something much more appalling came about before the emergence of two civilizations: the Western Empire simply disappeared. By 500, when the boundaries of the Eastern Empire were still much what they had been under Constantine, and his successors were still holding their own against the Persians, the last Western emperor had been deposed and his *insignia* sent to Constantinople by a barbarian king who claimed to rule as the Eastern emperor's representative in the West.

This is striking: what, actually, had collapsed? What had declined or fallen? Fifth-century writers bewailed it so much that it is easy to have the impression, heightened by such dramatic episodes as sackings of Rome itself, that the whole of society fell apart. This was not so. It was the state apparatus which collapsed, some of its functions ceasing to be carried out, and some passing into other hands. This was quite enough to explain the alarm. Institutions with a thousand years of history behind them gave way within a half-century. It is hardly surprising that people have asked why ever since.

One explanation is cumulative: the state

Djemila, a Christian enclave in present-day Algiers, was built in brick in the 5th and 6th centuries CE.

A rider in Germanic-style dress is shown setting out to go hunting in this mosaic from 6th-century CE Carthage. He may be a Vandal landowner who has adopted the customs of North Africa's romanized territory, captured from the empire in the 5th century.

apparatus in the West gradually seized up after the recovery of the fourth century. The whole concern became too big for the demographic, fiscal and economic base which carried it. The main purpose of raising revenue was to pay for the military machine, but it became more and more difficult to raise enough. There were no more conquests after Dacia to bring in new tribute. Soon the measures adopted to squeeze out more taxes drove rich and poor alike to devices for avoiding them. The effect was to make agricultural estates rely more and more upon meeting their own needs and becoming self-

supporting, rather than producing for the market. Parallel with this went a crumbling of urban government as trade languished and the rich withdrew to the countryside.

The military result was an army recruited from inferior material, because better could not be paid for. Even the reform of dividing it into mobile and garrison forces had its defects, for the first lost their fighting spirit by being stationed at the imperial residence and becoming used to the pampering and privileges that went with city postings, while the second turned into settled colonists, unwilling to take risks which would jeopardize their homesteads. Another descent in the unending spiral of decline logically followed. A weaker army drove the empire to rely still more on the very barbarians the army was supposed to keep at bay. As they had to be recruited as mercenaries, soothing and conciliatory politics were needed to keep them sweet. This led the Romans to concede more to the barbarians just when the pressure of the Germanic folk-movements was reaching a new climax. Migration and the attractive prospect of paid service with the empire probably counted for much more in the barbarian contribution to imperial collapse than the simple desire for loot. The prospect of booty might animate a raiding-party but could hardly bring down an empire.

THE GERMANIC THREAT

At the beginning of the fourth century Germanic peoples were stretched along the whole length of the frontier from the Rhine to the Black Sea, but it was in the south that the most formidable concentration was at that moment assembled. These were the Gothic peoples, Ostrogoth and Visigoth, who waited beyond the Danube. Some of them were already Christian, though in the Arian form. Together with Vandals, Burgundians and Lombards, they made up an east Germanic group. To the north were the west Germans: Franks, Alamanni, Saxons, Frisians and Thuringians. They would move into action in the second phase of the *Völkerwanderung* of the fourth and fifth centuries.

THE VISIGOTHS

The crisis began in the last quarter of the fourth century. The pressure on more western barbarians of the Huns, a formidable nomadic

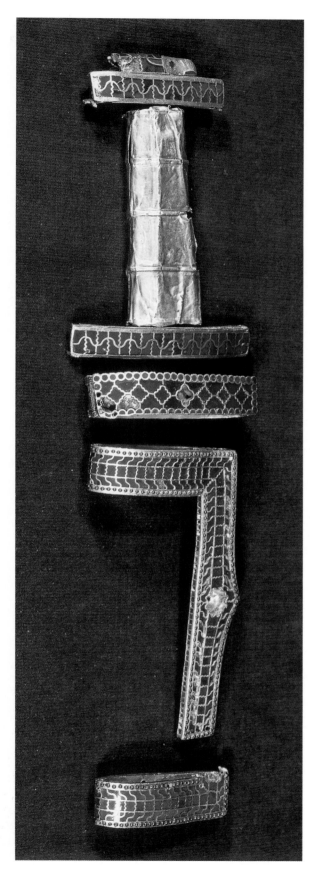

These are the decorated hilts of two swords found in the tomb of the Merovingian king Childeric, who died in 481 CE. Elaborately designed swords were used in Frankish countries until the 6th century. Gold inlay was characteristic of ornamental art from the East and was introduced to the West by the Germanic peoples.

The bas-reliefs on the Ludovisi sarcophagus, which dates from the 3rd century CE, depict scenes from battles between Romans and barbarians. The style is reminiscent of Hellenistic art: the sculptors' great skill and the theatricality of the composition serve to glorify the Roman legions' dead.

people from central Asia, was mounting after 370. They overran the Ostrogothic territory, defeated the Alans and then turned on the Visigoths near the Dniester. Unable to hold them, the Visigoths fled for refuge to the empire. In 376 they were allowed to cross the Danube to settle within the frontier. This was a new departure. Earlier barbarian incursions had been driven out or absorbed. Roman ways had attracted barbarian rulers and their followers had joined Rome's army. The Visigoths, though, came as a people, perhaps 40,000 strong, keeping their own laws and religion and remaining a compact unit. The emperor Valens intended to disarm them; it was not done and instead there was fighting. At the battle of Adrianople in 378 the emperor was killed and a Roman army defeated by the Visigoth cavalry. The Visigoths ravaged Thrace.

This was in more than one way a turning-point. Now whole tribes began to be enrolled as confederates – *foederati*, a word first used in 406 – and entered Roman territory to serve against other barbarians under their own chiefs. A temporary settlement with the Visigoths could not be maintained. The Eastern Empire was helpless to protect its European territories outside Constantinople, though when the Visigothic armies moved north towards Italy early in

Tacitus describes the German tribal warriors

"On the field of battle it is a disgrace to a chief to be surpassed in courage by his followers, and to the followers not to equal the courage of their chief. And to leave a battle alive after their chief has fallen means lifelong infamy and shame. To defend and protect him, and to let him get the credit for their own acts of heroism, are the most solemn obligations of their allegiance. The chiefs fight for victory, the followers for their chief. Many noble youths, if the land of their birth is stagnating in a long period of peace and inactivity, deliberately seek out other tribes which have some war in hand. For the Germans have no taste for peace; renown is more easily won among the perils, and a large body of retainers cannot be kept together except by means of violence and war. They are always making demands on the generosity of their chief, asking for a coveted war-horse or a spear stained with the blood of a defeated enemy. Their meals, for which plentiful if homely fare is provided, count in lieu of pay. The wherewithal for this openhandedness comes from war and plunder. A German is not so easily prevailed upon to plough the land and wait patiently for harvest as to challenge a foe and earn wounds for his reward. He thinks it tame and spiritless to accumulate slowly by the sweat of his brow what can be got quickly by the loss of a little blood."

An extract from *The Germania*, para 14, by Tacitus (c.56–c.120 CE), translated by H. Mattingly.

the fifth century, they were checked for a while by a Vandal general. By now the defence of Italy, the old heart of the empire, was entirely dependent on barbarian auxiliaries and soon even this was not enough; Constantinople might be held, but in 410 the Goths sacked Rome. After an abortive move to the south, with a view to pillaging Africa as they had pillaged Italy, the Visigoths again turned north, crossed the Alps into Gaul and eventually settled as the new kingdom of Toulouse in 419 CE, a Gothic state within the

This 6th-century CE belt buckle, made of gilded bronze and precious stones, is from the Visigothic kingdom in Spain.

The Eastern emperor Valens, depicted on this 4th-century CE gold coin, was far less talented than his brother, the Western emperor Valentinian I. Valens' poor judgment resulted in his army's defeat by the Visigoths – two-thirds of his troops died and the emperor was killed by a Visigothic arrow.

empire, where a Gothic aristocracy shared its overlordship with the old Gallo-Roman landlords.

THE GROWTH OF THE VANDAL KINGDOM

One other major movement of peoples still needs notice in order to explain the fifth-century remaking of the European racial and cultural map. In return for their settlement in Aquitania, the Western emperor had succeeded in getting the Visigoths to promise that they would help him to clear Spain of other barbarians. Of these the most important were the Vandals. In 406 the Rhine frontier, denuded of soldiers sent to defend Italy against the Visigoths, had given way too and the Vandals and Alans had broken into Gaul. From there they made their way southward, sacking and looting as they went and crossing the Pyrenees to establish a Vandal state in Spain. Twenty years later they were tempted to Africa by a dissident Roman governor who wanted their help. Visigoth attacks encouraged them to leave Spain. By 439 they had taken Carthage. The Vandal kingdom of Africa now had a naval base. They were to stay there for nearly a century and in 455 they, too, crossed to sack Rome and leave their name to history as a synonym for mindless destructiveness. Terrible as this was, though, it was less important than the seizure of Africa, the

mortal blow to the old Western Empire. It had now lost much of its economic base. Though great efforts could and would still be made in the West by Eastern emperors, Roman rule there was on its last legs. The dependence on one barbarian against another was a fatal handicap. The cumulative impact of fresh pressure made recovery impossible. The protection of Italy had meant abandoning Gaul and Spain to the Vandals; their invasion of Africa had meant the loss of Rome's grain-growing provinces.

This detail is taken from an illustration in the "Register of military and civil dignitaries", which was compiled in 390 CE. Africa is represented as the romanized granary of the empire: a woman is depicted holding ears of wheat and boats are shown transporting sacks of cereal.

This 396 CE diptych by Euquerius represents the Vandal Stilicho, the West's most important general. Stilicho exercised a kind of protectorate over the two emperors, Arcadius and Honorius, whose busts appear on his shield.

corridor of Asia peters out, he drove west for the last time with a huge army of allies, but was defeated near Troyes in 451 by a "Roman" army of Visigoths under a commander of barbarian origin. This was the end of the Hun threat; Attila died two years later, apparently scheming to marry the Western emperor's sister and perhaps become emperor himself. A great revolt the following year by the Huns' subjects in Hungary finally broke them and they are thenceforth almost lost to sight. In Asia, their home, new confederations of nomads were forming to play a similar part in the future, but their story can wait.

THE COLLAPSE OF THE WESTERN EMPIRE

The Huns had all but delivered the *coup de grâce* in the West; one emperor had sent the pope to intercede with Attila. The last Western emperor was deposed by a Germanic warlord, Odoacer, in 476 and formal sovereignty passed to the Eastern emperors. Though Italy, like the rest of the former Western provinces, was henceforth a barbarian kingdom, independent in all but name, Italians regarded the emperor as their sovereign, resident in Constantinople though he might be.

THE HUNS

The Western Empire's collapse was completed in Europe in the third quarter of the century. It followed the greatest of the Hun assaults. These nomads had followed the Germanic tribes into the Balkans and central Europe after a preliminary diversion to ravage Anatolia and Syria. By 440 the Huns were led by Attila, under whom their power was at its height. From Hungary, where the steppe

THE BARBARIANS' RISE TO POWER

The structure which had finally given way under these blows has in its last decades something of the Cheshire cat about it. It was fading away all the time; it is not particularly meaningful to pick one date rather than another as its end. It is unlikely that 476 seemed especially remarkable to contemporaries. The barbarian kingdoms were only a logical development of the reliance upon barbarian troops for the field army and their settlement as *foederati* within the frontiers. The barbarians themselves usually wanted no more, unless it was simple loot. Certainly they did not plan to replace imperial authority with their own. It is a Goth who is reported as saying, "I hope to go down to posterity as the restorer of Rome, since it is not possible that I should be its supplanter." Other dangers were greater and more fundamental than barbarian swagger.

Socially and economically, the tale of the third century had been resumed in the fifth. Cities decayed and population fell. The civil service slid deeper into disorder as officials sought to protect themselves against inflation by taking payment for carrying out their duties. Though revenue declined as provinces were lost, the sale of offices somehow kept up the lavish expenditure of the court. But independence of action was gone. From being emperors whose power rested on their armies, the last emperors of the West declined through the stage of being the equals in negotiation of barbarian warlords whom they had to placate, to being their puppets, cooped up in the last imperial capital, Ravenna. Contemporaries had been right in this sense to see the sack of Rome in 410 as the end of an age, for then it was revealed that the empire could no longer preserve the very heart of *romanitas*. By then, there had been many other signs, too, of what was going on. The last emperor of Constantine's house had tried during a brief reign (361–3) to restore the pagan cults; this had earned him historical fame (or, in Christian eyes, infamy) and, revealingly, the title "the Apostate", but he was not successful. Believing that a restoration of the old sacrifices would ensure the return of prosperity, he had too little time to test the proposition. What is now perhaps more striking is the unquestioned assumption that religion and public life were inseparably

This statue portrays Julian the Apostate, Roman emperor from 361 to 363 CE. Julian, who tried to revive paganism in the empire, wrote "We openly worship the gods and the bulk of the army which has followed me is full of piety. We sacrifice oxen in public; we have given thanks to the gods in numerous hecatombs. These gods order me to purify everything as much as possible and I devotedly obey." (Julian, *Letters*, XXVI)

This imposing silver plate, found in Spain, dates from the end of the 4th century CE and represents the court of Theodosius. The emperor, shown as a larger figure in the centre, is surrounded by the *caesars* and his sons Arcadius and Honorius, future emperors of the East and West respectively.

intertwined, on which his policy was based and which commanded general agreement; it was an assumption whose origins were Roman, not Christian. Julian did not threaten Constantine's work and Theodosius, the last ruler of a united empire, at last forbade the public worship of the ancient gods in 380.

THE REPRESSION OF PAGANISM

What the outlawing of ancient gods meant in practice is hard to say. In Egypt it seems to have been the final landmark in the process of overcoming the ancient civilization which had been going on for eight centuries or so. The victory of Greek ideas first won by the philosophers of Alexandria was now confirmed by the Christian clergy. The priests of the ancient cults were to be harried as pagans. Roman paganism found outspoken defenders still in the fifth century and only at the end of it were pagan teachers expelled from the universities at Athens and Constantinople. Nonetheless a great turning-point had been reached; in principle the closed Christian society of the Middle Ages was now in existence.

THE PERSECUTION OF THE JEWS

Christian emperors soon set about developing it in a particular direction which became only too familiar by depriving Jews, the most easily identifiable of groups alien to the closed society, of their juridical equality with other citizens. Here was another turning-point. Judaism had long been the only monotheistic representative in the pluralistic religious world of Rome and now it was ousted by its derivative, Christianity. A prohibition on proselytizing was the first blow and others soon followed. In 425 the patriarchate under which Jews had enjoyed administrative autonomy was abolished. When pogroms occurred, Jews began to withdraw to Persian territory. Their growing alienation from the empire weakened it, for they could soon call upon Rome's enemies for help. Jewish Arab states which lay along trade routes to Asia through the Red Sea were able to inflict damage on Roman interests in support of their co-religionists, too. Ideological rigour came at a high price.

THEODOSIUS

Theodosius' reign is also notable in Christian history because of his quarrel with St Ambrose, Bishop of Milan. In 390, after an insurrection at Thessalonica, Theodosius pitilessly massacred thousands of its inhabitants. To the amazement of contemporaries, the emperor was soon seen standing in penance

In this bas-relief from the obelisk in Constantinople's hippodrome, the emperor Theodosius and his family are shown attending chariot races.

Many beautiful Christian mosaics can be found in the city of Ravenna in Italy. This 5th-century CE mosaic is from the Mausoleum Galla Placidia and depicts Christ as the Good Shepherd watching over his flock.

This 4th-century CE Christian mosaic, which was originally a coffin cover, was found in a basilica in Tabarca, Tunisia. It features a representation of the basilica, surrounded by floral motifs and images of birds to symbolize paradise.

for the deed in a Milan church. Ambrose had refused him communion. Superstition had won the first round of what was to prove a long battle for humanity and enlightenment. Other men of might were to be tamed by excommunication or its threat, but this was the first time the spiritual arm had been so exercised and it is significant that it happened in the Western Church. Ambrose had alleged a higher duty for his office than that owed to the emperor. It is the inauguration of a great theme of western European history, the tension of spiritual and secular claims which was time and time again to pull it back into a progressive channel, the conflict of Church and State.

THE CHRISTIANIZATION OF THE EMPIRE

BY THE TIME ST AMBROSE refused to give communion to Theodosius, a glorious century for Christianity was almost over. It had been a great age of evangelization, in which missionaries had penetrated as far afield as Ethiopia, a brilliant age of theology and, above all, the age of establishment. Yet the Christianity of the age has about it much which now seems repellent and bilious. Establishment gave Christians power they did not hesitate to use. "We look on the same stars, the same heavens are above us all," pleaded one pagan to St Ambrose, "the same universe surrounds us. What matters it by what method each of us arrives at the truth?" But Symmachus asked in vain. East and West, the temper of the Christian Churches was intransigent and enthusiastic; if there was a distinction between the two, it lay between the Greeks' conviction of the almost limitless authority of a Christianized empire, blending spiritual and secular power, and the defensive, suspicious hostility to the whole secular world, state included, of a Latin tradition which taught Christians to see themselves as a saving remnant, tossed on the seas of sin and paganism in the Noah's Ark of the Church. Yet to be fair to the Fathers, or to understand their anxieties and fears, a modern observer has to recognize the compelling power of superstition and mystery in the whole late classical world. Christianity acknowledged and expressed it. The demons among whom Christians walked their earthly ways were real to them and to pagans alike, and a fifth-century pope consulted the augurs in order to find out what to do about the Goths.

RIVAL RELIGIONS

The power of superstition is part of the explanation of the bitterness with which heresy and schism were pursued. Arianism had not been finished off at Nicaea; it flourished among the Gothic peoples and Arian Christianity was dominant over much of Italy, Gaul and Spain. The Catholic Church was not persecuted in the Arian barbarian kingdoms, but it was neglected there and when everything depended on the patronage of rulers and the great, neglect could be dangerous. Another threat was the Donatist schism in Africa, which had taken on a social content and broke out in violent conflicts of town and country. In Africa, too, the old threat of Gnosticism lived again in Manichaeism which came to the West from Persia; another heresy, Pelagianism, showed the readiness of some Christians in Latinized Europe to welcome a version of Christianity which subordinated mystery and sacramentalism to the aim of living a good life.

THE LIFE OF ST AUGUSTINE OF HIPPO

FEW MEN were better fitted by temperament or education to discern, analyse and combat such dangers than was St Augustine, the greatest of the Fathers. It was important that he came from Africa – that is to say, the Roman province of that name, which corresponded roughly to Tunisia and eastern Algeria – where he was born in 354. African Christianity had more than a century's life behind it by then but was still a minority affair. The African Church had had a special temper of its own since the days of Tertullian, its great founding figure. Its roots did not lie in the Hellenized cities of the East, but in soil laid down by the religions of Carthage and

St Ambrose, Bishop of Milan in the late 4th century CE, was one of the original four Doctors of the Church and had an enormous influence on the development of the Church.

Numidia which lingered on amid the Berber peasantry. The humanized deities of Olympus had never been at home in Africa. The local traditions were of remote gods dwelling in high places, worshipped in savage and ecstatic rituals (the Carthaginians are supposed to have practised child sacrifice).

AUGUSTINE'S SPIRITUALITY

The intransigent, violent temper of the African Christianity which grew up against this background was reflected to the full in Augustine's own personality. He responded to the same psychological stimuli and felt the

Among the many diverse early Christian cults that were in existence around the time of St Augustine, the Copts were an important group. This Coptic linen cloth was produced in Egypt in the 4th or 5th century CE. The figure is wearing a pointed cap – a style imported to the region from western Asia – to symbolize his divinity or heroism.

The church of San Lorenzo in Milan was built in the 4th and 5th centuries CE on a square base, with a central dome and four elevated towers on the corners. The building, the interior of which is seen here, was probably originally used to house the imperial family's tombs.

need to confront the fact of an evil lurking in himself. One answer was available and popular. The stark dualism of Manichaeism had a very wide appeal in Africa; Augustine was a Manichee for nearly ten years. Characteristically, he then reacted against his errors with great violence.

Before adulthood and Manichaeism, Augustine's education had orientated him towards a public career in the Western Empire. That education was overwhelmingly Latin (Augustine probably spoke only that language and certainly found Greek difficult) and very selective. Its skills were those of rhetoric and it was in them that Augustine first won prizes, but as for ideas, it was barren. Augustine taught himself by reading; his first great step forward was the discovery of the works of Cicero, probably his first contact, though at secondhand, with the classical Athenian tradition.

BAPTISM

Augustine's lay career ended in Milan (where he had gone to teach rhetoric) with his baptism as a Catholic by St Ambrose himself in 387. At that time Ambrose exercised an authority which rivalled that of the empire itself in one of its most important cities. Augustine's observation of this relation between religion and secular power confirmed him in views very different from those of Greek churchmen, who welcomed the conflation of lay and religious authority in the emperor which followed establishment. Augustine then returned to Africa, first to live as a monk at Hippo and then, reluctantly, to become its bishop. There he remained until his death in 430, building up Catholicism's position against the Donatists and, thanks to a huge literary output, becoming a dominant personality of the Western Church.

These are the ruins of a Roman Christian enclave in Tebessa, in present-day Algeria. The settlement dates from the 5th and 6th centuries CE.

AUGUSTINE AND THEOLOGY

In his lifetime Augustine was best known for his attacks on the Donatists and the Pelagians. The first was really a political question: which of two rival Churches was to dominate Roman Africa? The second raised wider issues. They must seem remote to our non-theologically minded age but on them turned much future European history. Essentially, the Pelagians preached a kind of Stoicism; they were part of the classical world and tradition, dressed up in Christian theological language though it might be. The danger this presented – if it was a danger – was that the distinctiveness of Christianity would be lost and the Church simply become the vehicle of one strain in classical Mediterranean civilization, with the strengths and weaknesses which that implied. Augustine was uncompromisingly other-worldly and theological; for him the only possibility of redemption for humanity lay in the Grace which God conferred and no human being could command by his or her works. In the history of the human spirit Augustine deserves a place for having laid out more comprehensively than any predecessor the lines of the great debate between predestination and free will, Grace and Works, belief and motive, which was to run for so long through European history. Almost incidentally, he established Latin Christianity firmly on the rock of the Church's unique power of access to the source of Grace through the sacraments.

AUGUSTINE'S WRITINGS

The detail of the voluminous writing of St Augustine (as he came to be) is now largely neglected except by specialists. Instead, he now enjoys instead some notoriety as one of the most forceful and insistent exponents of a distrust of the flesh which was long especially to mark Christian sexual attitudes and thereby the whole of Western culture. He stands in strange company – with Plato, for example – as a founding father of puritanism. But his intellectual legacy was far richer than this suggests. In his writings can also be seen the foundations of much medieval political thought in so far as they are not Aristotelian or legalistic, and a view of history which would long dominate Christian society in the West and would affect it as importantly as the words of Christ himself.

The book now called *The City of God*

This is an illuminated page from St Augustine's manuscript *The City of God*. Augustine (354–430 CE) converted to Christianity when he was 32 years old and was baptized in Milan by St Ambrose.

contains the writing of Augustine which had most future impact. It is not so much a matter of specific ideas or doctrines – there is difficulty in locating his precise influence on medieval political thinkers, perhaps because there is much ambiguity about what he says – as of an attitude. He laid out in this book a way of looking at history and the government of the human race which became inseparable from Christian thinking for a thousand years and more. The subtitle of the book is *Against the Pagans*. This reveals his aim: to refute the reactionary and pagan charge that the troubles crowding in on the empire were to be blamed on Christianity. He was inspired to write by the Gothic sack of

The chair of Archbishop Maximian was made in the 6th century for the church of St Vitale in Ravenna. On the front St John the Baptist appears with the four Evangelists.

Rome in 410; his overriding aim was to demonstrate that the understanding of even such an appalling event was possible for a Christian and, indeed, could only be understand through the Christian religion, but his huge book swoops far and wide over the past, from the importance of chastity to the philosophy of Thales of Miletus, and expounds the civil wars of Marius and Sulla as carefully as the meaning of God's promises to David. It is impossible to summarize: "It may be too much for some, too little for others," said Augustine wryly in his last paragraph. It is a Christian interpretation of a whole civilization and what went to its making. Its most remarkable feature is its own central judgment: that the whole earthly tissue of things is dispensable, and culture and institutions – even the great empire itself – of no final value, if God so wills.

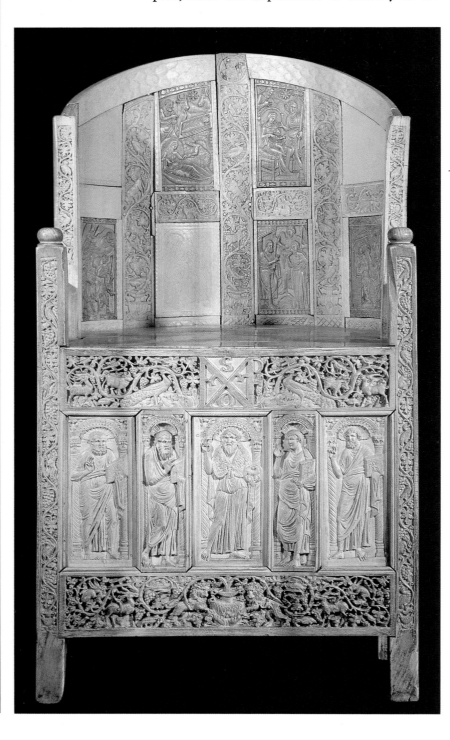

THE TWO CITIES

That God did so will was suggested by Augustine's central image of two cities. One was earthly, founded in human beings' lower nature, imperfect and made with sinful hands, however glorious its appearance and however important the part it might from time to time have to play in the divine scheme. Sometimes its sinful aspect predominates and it is clear that humanity must flee the earthly city – but Babylon, too, had had its part in the divine plan. The other city was the heavenly city of God, the community founded on the assurance of God's promise of salvation, a goal towards which the human race might make a fearful pilgrimage from the earthly city, led and inspired by the Church. In the Church was to be found both the symbol of the City of God and the means of reaching it. History had changed with the appearance of the Church: from that moment the struggle of good and evil was clear in the world and human salvation rested upon its defence. Such arguments would be heard long into modern times.

The two cities sometimes make other appearances in Augustine's argument, too. They are sometimes two groups of men, those who are condemned to punishment in the next world and those who are making the pilgrimage to glory. At this level the cities are divisions of the actual human race, here and now, as well as of all those since Adam who have already passed to judgment. But Augustine did not think that membership of the Church explicitly defines one group, the rest of humanity being the other. Perhaps the power of Augustine's vision was all the greater because of its ambiguities, dangling threads of argument and suggestion. The state was not *merely*

The above coin bears the effigy of Romulus Augustus, the last Western Roman emperor to be officially recognized. He was deposed by the barbarian general Odoacer in 476 CE, signalling the end of the classical age in the West.

earthly and wicked: it had its role in the divine scheme and government, in its nature, was divinely given. Much was later to be heard about that; the state would be asked to serve the Church by preserving it from its carnal enemies and by using its own power to enforce the purity of the Faith. Yet the Mandate of Heaven (as another civilization might put it) could be withdrawn and, when it was, even an event like the sack of Rome was only a landmark in the working of judgment on sin. In the end the City of God would prevail.

The sides and lid of this marble shrine are decorated with exquisite bas-reliefs portraying biblical scenes. Medallions depicting Christ and the Apostles line the edge of the lid. The shrine was probably produced in a Milanese workshop in the mid-4th century CE.

THE LEGACY OF ST AUGUSTINE

St Augustine escapes simple definition in his greatest book but perhaps he escapes it in every sense. Much remains to be said about him for which there is little room here. He was, for example, a careful and conscientious bishop, the loving pastor of his flock; he was also a persecutor with the dubious distinction of having persuaded the imperial government to use force against the Donatists. He wrote a fascinating spiritual study which, though profoundly misleading on the facts of his early life, virtually founded the literary genre of romantic and introspective autobiography.

He could be an artist with words – Latin ones, not Greek (he had to ask St Jerome for help with Greek translation) – and a prize-winning scholar, but his artistry was born of passion rather than of craftsmanship and his Latin is often poor. Yet he was soaked in the classical Roman past. It was from the high ground of his mastery of this tradition that he looked out with the eyes of Christian faith to a cloudy, uncertain and, in others' eyes, frightening future. He embodied two cultures more completely, perhaps, than any other man of those divided times and perhaps this is why, fifteen hundred years later, he still seems to dominate them.

St Augustine's disciples are depicted in this illustration from an Anglo-Saxon manuscript of the saint's greatest work, *The City of God.*

5 THE ELEMENTS OF A FUTURE

Britain's many surviving Roman ruins serve as reminders of its time under the rule of the empire. This lighthouse, which overlooks the English Channel at Dover in Kent, was built by the Romans in the 1st or 2nd century CE.

FROM THE GERMANIC INVASIONS grew in the end the first nations of modern Europe, but when the Western Empire disappeared the barbarian peoples did not occupy areas looking much like later states. They fall clearly into four major and distinctive groups. The northernmost, the Saxons, Angles and Jutes, were moving into the old Roman province of Britain from the fourth century onwards, well before the island was abandoned to its inhabitants when the last emperor to be proclaimed there by his soldiers crossed with his army to Gaul in 407. Britain was then contested between successive waves of invaders and the Romano-British inhabitants until there emerged from it at the beginning of the seventh century a group of seven Anglo-Saxon kingdoms fringed by a Celtic world consisting of Ireland, Wales and Scotland.

THE END OF ROMANO-BRITISH CIVILIZATION

Although the first British still lived on in communities which seem to have survived sometimes to the tenth century, and perhaps longer, Romano-British civilization disappeared more completely than its equivalents anywhere else in the Western Empire. Even the language was to go; a Germanic tongue almost completely replaced it. We may have a fleeting glimpse of the last spasms of Romano-British resistance in the legend of King Arthur and his knights, which could be a reminiscence of the cavalry-fighting skills of the late imperial army, but that is all. Of administrative or spiritual continuity between

Time chart (419 CE–604 CE)							
						527–565 CE Reign of the emperor Justinian; codification of Roman law. Temporary reunification of large part of the old Roman Empire	587 CE The Visigoth king Recared converts to Catholicism
400 CE	450 CE	475 CE	500 CE	525 CE	550 CE		600 CE
	419 CE The Visigoth kingdom of Toulouse is founded		496 CE The Frankish king Clovis converts to Catholicism	507 CE The Visigoth kingdom in Spain is founded	526 CE The Ostrogoth king Theodoric dies	529 CE St Benedict of Nursia establishes his monastic order in the West	590–604 CE Gregory the Great is pope

493 CE The Italian Ostrogoth kingdom is founded

this imperial province and the barbarian kingdoms there is virtually no trace. The imperial heritage of the future England was purely physical. It lay in the ruins of towns and villas, occasional Christian crosses, or the great constructions like Hadrian's Wall which were to puzzle newcomers until they came at last to believe that they were the work of giants of superhuman power. Some of these relics, like the complex of baths built upon the thermal springs at Bath, disappeared from sight for hundreds of years until rediscovered by the antiquaries of the eighteenth and nineteenth centuries. The roads remained, sometimes serving for centuries as trade routes even when their engineering had succumbed to time, weather and pillage. Finally, there were the natural immigrants who had come with the Romans and stayed: animals like ferrets, or plants like mustard, which was to spice the roast beef that became a minor national mythology over a thousand years later. But of the things of the mind left by the Romans we have hardly a trace. Romano-British Christianity, whatever it may have been, disappeared and the keepers of the faith retired for a time to the misty fastnesses where there brooded the monks of the Celtic Church. It was another Rome which was to convert the English nation, not the empire. Before that, Germanic tradition would be the preponderant formative influence as nowhere else within the old imperial territory.

THE FRANKS

ACROSS THE CHANNEL, things were very different. Much survived. After its devastation by the Vandals, Gaul continued to lie in the shadow of the Visigoths of Aquitaine. Their share in repelling the Huns gave them greater importance than ever. To the northeast of Gaul, nevertheless, lay German tribes which were to displace them from this superiority, the Franks. Unlike the Visigoths, they were not Arian and in part because of this the future was to belong to them. They were to have a bigger impact on the shaping of Europe than any other barbarian people.

The graves of the first Franks reveal a warrior society, divided into a hierarchy of

The growth of the Frankish kingdom

Of all the Germanic peoples, the Franks had the greatest influence on the formation of the future Europe. In the 4th century, they were already established in the region of present-day Belgium, where many of them became federal Roman soldiers. Some Franks eventually emigrated southward and established themselves in Gaul itself. One group, based in Tournai, founded the Merovingian Dynasty – their third king, Clovis, expanded the kingdom's territory and moved the capital to Paris. He was married to a princess from Burgundy and converted to Catholicism in 496 – a decision that gained him the support of the Roman Church and the friendship of the Gallo-Roman people. At the end of the 6th century, the Frankish kingdom included former Germanic lands such as Austrasia, the centre of which was located in the Rhine valley, where most of the Franks now lived.

Having become one of the most powerful peoples in the empire, the Franks also began to conquer romanized lands, mainly inhabited by Latin-speaking people. They took Neustria in the Seine valley in the 5th century and Burgundy in the Rhône valley in the middle of the 6th century. At this time, the Frankish kingdom was already a Latinized state, with a settled population and a large number of noble landowners.

Dating from the 7th century, this Frankish stone funerary monument features a stylized figure of Christ.

This engraved wooden writing desk was commissioned by Queen Radegunda in the 6th century. Radegunda, who was later canonized, was married to the Frankish king Chlotar I but left him to become a nun.

ranks. More willing to settle than some other barbarians, they were established in the fourth century in modern Belgium, between the Scheldt and the Meuse, where they became Roman *foederati*. Some of them moved on into Gaul. One group, settled at Tournai, threw up a ruling family subsequently called Merovingians; the third king (if this is the correct word) of this line was Clovis. His is the first great name in the history of the country known as Francia after the peoples which Clovis put together.

CLOVIS

Clovis became ruler of the western Franks in 481. Though formally the subject of the emperor, he soon turned on the last Roman governors of Gaul and conquered lands far to the west and down to the Loire. Meanwhile the eastern Franks defeated the Alamanni and when Clovis had been elected their king, too, a united Frankish kingdom straddled the lower Rhine valley and northern France. This was the heartland of the Frankish state which was the heir to Roman supremacy in north Europe. Clovis married a princess from

another Germanic people, the Burgundians, who had settled in the Rhône valley and the area running southeast to modern Geneva and Besançon. She was a Catholic, though her people were Arians, and at some time after their marriage (traditionally in 496) and after a battlefield conversion which is reminiscent of Constantine's, Clovis himself embraced Catholicism. This gave him the support of the Roman Church, the most important power still surviving from the empire in the barbarian lands, in what it now chose to regard as a religious war against the other Germanic peoples of Gaul. Catholicism was also the way to friendship with the Romano-Gaulish population. No doubt the conversion was political; it was also momentous. A new Rome was to rule in Gaul.

The Burgundians were Clovis' first victims, though they were not subjugated completely until after his death, when they were given Merovingian princes but kept an independent state structure. The Visigoths were tackled next; they were left only the southeastern territories they held north of the Pyrenees (the later Languedoc and Roussillon and Provence). Clovis was now the successor of the Romans in all Gaul;

the emperor recognized it by naming him a consul.

The Frankish capital was moved to Paris by Clovis and he was buried in the church he had built there, the first Frankish king not to be buried as a barbarian. But this was not the start of the continuous history of Paris as a capital. A Germanic kingdom was not what later times would think of as a state nor what a Roman would recognize. It was a heritage composed partly of lands, partly of kinship groups. Clovis' heritage was divided among his sons. The Frankish kingdom was not reunited until 558. A couple of years later it broke up again. Gradually, it settled down in three bits. One was Austrasia, with its capital at Metz and its centre of gravity east of the Rhine; Neustria was the western equivalent and had its capital at Soissons; under the same ruler, but distinct, was the kingdom of Burgundy. Their rulers tended to quarrel over the lands where these regions touched.

A bearded head of Christ is the centrepiece of this round silver clasp, decorated with small garnet incrustations. Frankish in origin, it dates from the 6th or 7th century.

THE EARLY FRANKISH NATION

In this tripartite structure there begins to appear a Frankish nation no longer a collection of barbarian war bands, but peoples belonging to a recognizable state, speaking a Latin vernacular, and with an emerging class of landowning nobles. Significantly, from it there also comes a Christian interpretation of the barbarian role in history, the *History of the Franks*, by Gregory, Bishop of Tours, himself from the Romano-Gaulish aristocracy. Other barbarian peoples would produce similar works (the greatest, perhaps, is that written for England by the Venerable Bede) which sought to reconcile traditions in which paganism was still strong to Christianity and the civilized heritage. It must be said that Gregory presented a picture of the Franks after the death of his hero Clovis which was pessimistic; he thought the Frankish rulers had behaved so badly that their kingdom was doomed.

KING THEODORIC

The Merovingians kept other barbarians out of Gaul, and took their lands north of the Alps from the Ostrogoths, where their greatest king was Theodoric. His right to rule in Italy, where he fought off other Germans, was recognized by the emperor in 497. He was utterly convinced of Rome's authority; he had an emperor as godfather and had been brought up at Constantinople until he was eighteen. "Our royalty is an imitation of yours, a copy of the only empire on earth," he once wrote to the emperor in Constantinople from his capital in Ravenna. On his coins appeared the legend "Unvanquished Rome" (*Roma invicta*), and when he went to Rome, Theodoric held games in the old style in the circus. Yet

Anicius Manlius Severinus Boethius, consul in 510, is depicted on this marble diptych. Boethius lived during the reign of Theodoric and made significant contributions to the fields of theology, philosophy, science and music.

technically he was the only Ostrogoth who was a Roman citizen, his authority accepted by the Senate; his countrymen were merely the mercenary soldiers of the empire. To civil offices he appointed Romans. One of them was his friend and adviser, the philosopher Boethius, who was to be possibly the most important single channel through which the legacy of the classical world passed to medieval Europe.

Theodoric seems to have been a judicious ruler, maintaining good relations with other barbarian peoples (he married Clovis' sister) and enjoying some sort of primacy among them. But he did not share his own people's Arian faith, and religious division told against Ostrogothic power in the long run. Unlike the Franks, and in spite of their ruler's

The Ostrogoths, having established themselves in northern Italy in 488, introduced a highly colourful style of gold- and silverwork. This clasp, dating from 500, is made of gold studded with emeralds and other small stones. The upper part is decorated with four eagles' heads.

example, they were not to ally with the Roman past; and after Theodoric the Ostrogoths were expelled from Italy and history by the generals from the Eastern Empire. They left a ruined Italy, soon to be invaded by yet another barbarian people, the Lombards.

VISIGOTHIC SPAIN

In the west Clovis had left the Visigoths virtually confined to Spain, from which they had driven the Vandals. Other Germanic peoples were already settled there. Its terrain presented quite special problems – as it has continued to do to all invaders and governments – and the Visigothic kingdom of Spain was not able to resist much more romanization than its founders had undergone in Gaul, where they had fused much less with existing society than had the Franks. The Visigoths – and there were not so very many of them, less than 100,000 at most – clustered about their leaders who spread out from Old Castile through the provinces; they then quarrelled so much that imperial rule was able to re-establish itself for more than a half-century in the south. Finally, the Visigothic kings turned to Catholicism and thus enlisted the authority of the Spanish bishops. In 587 begins the long tradition of Catholic monarchy in Spain.

ROMAN AND BARBARIAN WESTERN EUROPE

What the flux of peoples in Europe adds up to is hard to say. Generalization is hazardous. Simple duration alone almost explains this; the Visigoths underwent three centuries of evolution between the creation of the kingdom of Toulouse and the end of their ascendancy in Spain. Much changed in so long a time.

Theodoric, King of the Ostrogoths, was buried in 526 in this mausoleum outside the city walls of Ravenna. The stone building is crowned with a huge monolith and is similar in style to many Roman funerary monuments.

Though economic life and technology hardly altered, mental and institutional forms were undergoing radical, if slow, transformations in all the barbarian kingdoms. Soon it is not quite right to think of them still as merely such (except, perhaps, the Lombards). The Germanic population were a minority, often isolated in alien settings, dependent on routines long established by the particular environment for their living and forced into some sort of understanding with the conquered. The passage of their invasions must sometimes have seemed at close quarters like a flood tide, but when it had passed there were often only tiny, isolated pools of invaders left behind, here and there replacing the Roman masters, but often living alongside them and with them. Marriage between Roman and barbarian was not legal until the sixth century, but that was not much of a check. In Gaul the Franks took up its Latin, adding Frankish words to it. By the seventh century, western European society has already

The Visigoths

The presence of the Visigoth Germanic people was first recorded in Gaul. There they founded a kingdom, with its capital at Toulouse, which lasted from 419 to 457, the year in which the Franks seized southern Gaul. From this time the Visigoths, who probably numbered only 100,000 in total, moved to establish themselves in the centre of the Iberian peninsula, between the Ebro and the Tagus rivers, where the population of Hispano-Roman people was least dense. At the end of the 6th century, they conquered the Swabian kingdom in the northwest of the country, which had been established at the beginning of the previous century, and made Toledo their capital. Lengthy internal disputes in the middle of the 6th century led to the establishment of imperial Byzantine control in the south, as a result of the campaign by the emperor Justinian to restore the old Roman Empire.

The Visigoths, like many of the Germanic peoples who had been Christianized in early times, were Arians. In the year 587, however, their king, Recared, converted to Roman Catholicism, as the Frankish king Clovis had done almost a century earlier. The Visigoth kingdom assimilated many aspects of Roman culture and tradition and, at the end of the 7th century, a Romano–Visigoth code was set up – clear evidence of the cultural changes that had taken place within the kingdom. Visigoth power in the old Hispania disappeared in 711 with the arrival of the Muslims.

A capital from the church of San Pedro de la Nave near Zamora, Spain. Carved by skilful stonemasons in the 7th century, the scene represents the biblical story of Daniel in the lions' den. In the abacus, top, the intricate decoration with plant-like spirals includes images of birds and fruit.

This marble diptych depicts a Roman consul in the Ostrogoth kingdom in 530, Rufus Genadius Probus Orestes. He appears in his consular garments, seated on a throne and accompanied by two figures representing Rome and Constantinople. Above his head are the busts of the Ostrogoth king Athalaric and his mother Amalasuntha. The piece symbolizes the Ostrogoth leaders' goodwill towards Rome and their desire that there should be harmony between East and West.

a very different atmosphere from that of the turbulent fifth.

GERMANIC CULTURAL LEGACY

The barbarian past left its imprint. In almost all the barbarian kingdoms society was long and irreversibly shaped by Germanic custom. This sanctioned a hierarchy reflected in the characteristic Germanic device for securing public order, the blood feud. Men – and women, and cattle, and property of all sorts – had in the most literal sense their price; wrongs done were settled by interesting a whole clan or family in the outcome if customary compensation were not forthcoming. Kings more and more wrote down and thus in

a sense "published" what such customs were. Literacy was so rare that there can have been no point in imagining devices such as the stele of Babylon or the white boards on which the decrees of Greek city-states were set out. Recording by a scribe on parchment for future consultation was all that could be envisaged. None the less, in this Germanic world lie the origins of a jurisprudence one day to be carried across oceans to new cultures of European stock. The first institution to open the way to this was the acceptance of kingly or collective power to declare what was to be recorded. All the Germanic kingdoms moved towards the writing down and codification of their law.

THE BARBARIANS AND THE ROMAN TRADITION

Where the early forms of public action are not religious or supernatural, they are usually judicial, and it is hardly surprising that, for example, the Visigothic court of Toulouse should have sought the skills of Roman legal experts. But this was only one form of a respect which almost every barbarian aristocracy showed for Roman tradition and forms. Theodoric saw himself as the representative of the emperor; his problem did not lie in identifying his own role, but in the need to avoid irritating his followers who could be provoked by any excess of romanization. Perhaps similar considerations weighed with Clovis before his conversion, which was an act of identification with empire as well as with Church. At the level just below such heroic figures, both Frankish and Visigothic noblemen seem to have taken pleasure in showing themselves the heirs of Rome by writing to one another in Latin and patronizing light literature. There was a tie of interest with the Romans, too; Visigothic warriors

sometimes found employment in putting down the revolts of peasants who menaced the Romano-Gaulish landowner as well as the invaders. Yet so long as Arianism stood in the way, there was a limit to the identification with *romanitas* possible for the barbarians. The Church, after all, was the supreme relic of empire west of Constantinople.

The Eastern emperors had not seen these changes with indifference. But troubles in their own domains hamstrung them and in the fifth century their barbarian generals dominated them too. They watched with apprehension the last years of the puppet emperors of Ravenna but recognized Odoacer, the deposer of the last of them. They maintained a formal claim to rule over a single empire, east and west, without actually questioning Odoacer's independence in Italy until an effective replacement was available in Theodoric, to whom the title of patrician was given. Meanwhile, Persian wars and the new pressure of Slavs in the Balkans were more than enough to deal with. It was not until the accession of the emperor Justinian in 527 that it seemed likely that reality would be restored to imperial government.

JUSTINIAN

IN RETROSPECT JUSTINIAN SEEMS something of a failure. Yet he behaved as people thought an emperor should; he did what most people still expected that a strong emperor would one day do. He boasted that Latin was his native tongue; for all the wide sweep of the empire's foreign relations, he could still think plausibly of reuniting and restoring the old empire, centred on Constantinople though it now had to be. We labour under the handicap of knowing what happened, but he reigned a long time and his contemporaries were more struck by his temporary successes. They expected them to herald a real restoration. After all, no one could really conceive a world without the empire. The barbarian kings of the West gladly deferred to Constantinople and accepted titles from it;

Justinian's empire 527–565 CE

On his accession to the imperial throne in 527, Justinian embarked on a series of military campaigns, with the objective of reunifying and restoring the former Roman Empire. For a few years, as a result of Justinian's conquests, the Byzantine dominions were extended to North Africa, southern Spain and Italy: once again, large areas of the Mediterranean coast were united to form a single state. However, the unity restored by Justinian was destroyed again at the end of the 6th century by the unstoppable advances of the Germanic and Slavic peoples, and in the 7th century by the expansion of Islam.

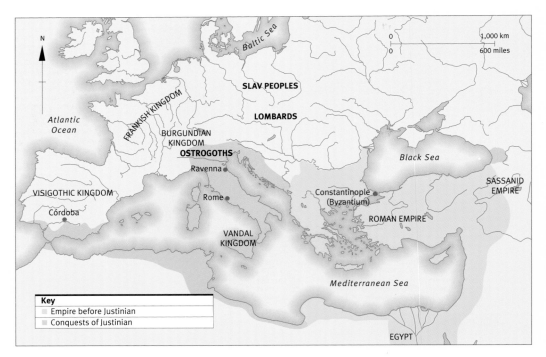

The above map shows the extent of the Byzantine Empire at the time of Justinian's accession and the territories he added during his long reign.

In this mosaic from the church of St Vitale in Ravenna, Justinian is shown with his retinue of ecclesiastical dignitaries and courtiers. The halo around Justinian's head is a reminder of the emperor's sacred status. While the figures' faces are individual and expressive, their bodies give the impression of floating in space, emphasizing their spirituality.

they did not grasp at the purple themselves. Justinian sought autocratic power, and his contemporaries found the goal both comprehensible and realistic. There is a certain grandeur about his conception of his role; it is a pity that he should have been so unattractive a man.

Justinian was almost always at war. Often he was victorious. Even the costly Persian campaigns (and payments to the Persian king) were successful in the limited sense that they did not lose the empire much ground.

Yet they were a grave strategic handicap; the liberation of his resources for a policy of recovery in the West which had been Justinian's aim in his first peace with the Persians always eluded him. Nevertheless, his greatest general, Belisarius, destroyed Vandal Africa and recovered that country for the empire (though it took ten years to reduce it to order). He went on to invade Italy and begin the struggle which ended in 554 with the final eviction of the Ostrogoths from Rome and the unification once more of all

This is the front of a 7th-century helmet that is thought to have belonged to Agilulf, who was King of the Lombards between 590 and 615. In spite of the crudeness of the reliefs, the Roman influence is evident in the warriors' appearance and in the figures of winged victories watching over the monarch.

Justinian, Emperor of the East from 527 to 565, did everything in his power to reunite the old Roman Empire. Although his success was short-lived, Justinian left a remarkable legacy, including numerous civic and religious buildings and the codification of Roman law (a major contribution to the development of the modern idea of the state).

Byzantine architecture

The people of the Byzantine Empire inherited their taste for grandiose architecture from ancient Rome. The Byzantines also developed an ever-greater passion for decorative richness and the use of polychromy through their close contact with the East. Amid the rigidity and pomp of court ceremonies, the emperor's public appearances were carefully and elaborately staged to set him apart from ordinary mortals and make him seem nearer to the divine world. This sumptuous theatricality had an important influence on the artistic tastes of the period and inspired the magnificence of Byzantine buildings. The Eastern Roman Empire's architectural style was not totally formed until the time of Justinian, in the 6th century. The emperor adapted the region's existing vaulted architecture and sought to create a new architectural style suitable for his holy realm, leaving a legacy of sumptuous imperial palaces and beautiful churches.

The major features of Byzantine architecture were the prominence of domes and capitals and the use of mosaics as a decoration for the walls rather than the floors, as had been the Roman custom. The Byzantines managed to build domes of huge proportions, such as that of St Sophia in Constantinople, which is more than 100 ft (30 m) in diameter. Byzantine capitals, based on the Roman Corinthian style, were converted into truncated structures decorated with luxuriant foliage. Highly skilled Byzantine artists covered the churches' walls and vaults with brightly coloured mosaics depicting emperors, saints and ecclesiastical dignitaries or scenes from the Bible.

The major Byzantine monuments to have been preserved can be found in Constantinople itself (now Istanbul) and in Ravenna, capital of the exarchate, which included the imperial domain that Justinian restored in Italy, Spain and North Africa.

Depicting the port of Classe, this mosaic from the St Apollinaris basilica near Ravenna dates from the 6th century. As in many Byzantine mosaics, the use of gold creates an impression of grandeur.

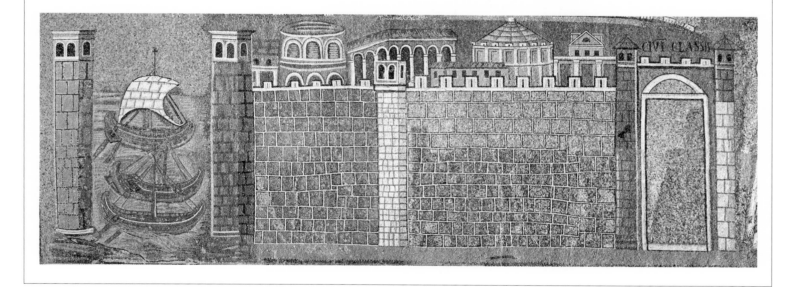

Italy under imperial rule, albeit an Italy devastated by the imperial armies as it had never been by the barbarians. These were great achievements, though badly followed up. More were to follow in southern Spain, where the imperial armies exploited rivalry between Visigoths and again set up imperial government in Córdoba. Throughout the western Mediterranean, too, the imperial fleets were supreme; for a century after

Justinian's death, Byzantine ships moved about unmolested.

It did not last. By the end of the century most of Italy was gone again, this time to the Lombards, another Germanic people and the final extinguishers of imperial power in the peninsula. In eastern Europe, too, in spite of a vigorous diplomacy of bribery and missionary ideology, Justinian had never been successful in dealing with the barbarians.

The magnificent church of St Sophia in Constantinople, which later became a mosque, was consecrated in 537. It has a large central dome supported by pillars, arches and secondary vaulting. This immense space is enhanced by the play of light through the building's many windows.

Perhaps enduring success there was impossible. The pressure from behind on these migrant peoples was too great and, besides, they could see great prizes ahead; "the barbarians," wrote one historian of the reign, "having once tasted Roman wealth, never forgot the road that led to it." By Justinian's death, in spite of his expensive fortress-building, the ancestors of the later Bulgars were settled in Thrace and a wedge of barbarian peoples separated West and East Rome.

JUSTINIAN'S LEGACY

Justinian's conquests, great as they were, could not be maintained by his successors in the face of the continuing threat from Persia,

the rise of Slav pressure in the Balkans and, in the seventh century, a new rival, Islam. A terrible time lay ahead. Yet even then Justinian's legacy would be operative through the diplomatic tradition he founded, the building of a network of influences among the barbarian peoples beyond the frontier, playing off one against another, bribing one prince with tribute or a title, standing godparent to the baptized children of a second. If it had not been for the client princedoms of the Caucasus who were converted to Christianity in Justinian's day, or his alliance with the Crimean Goths (which was to last seven centuries), the survival of the Eastern Empire would have been almost impossible. In this sense, too, the reign sets out the ground-plan of a future Byzantine sphere.

Within the empire, Justinian left an indelible imprint. At his accession the monarchy was handicapped by the persistence of party rivalries which could draw upon popular support, but in 532 this led to a great insurrection which made it possible to strike at the factions and, though much of the city was burned, this was the end of domestic threats to Justinian's autocracy. It showed itself henceforth more and more consistently and nakedly.

Its material monuments were lavish; the greatest is the basilica of St Sophia itself (532–7 CE), but all over the empire public buildings, churches, baths and new towns mark the reign and speak for the inherent wealth of the Eastern Empire. The richest and most civilized provinces were in Asia and Egypt; Alexandria, Antioch and Beirut were their great cities. A nonmaterial, institutional monument of the reign was Justinian's codification of Roman law. In four collections a thousand years of Roman jurisprudence was put together in a form which gave it deep influence across the centuries and helped to shape the modern idea of the state.

Justinian's efforts to win administrative and organizational reform were far less successful. It was not difficult to diagnose ills known to be dangerous as long before as the third century. But given the expense and responsibilities of empire, permanent remedies were hard to find. The sale of offices, for example, was known to be an evil and Justinian abolished it, but then had to tolerate it when it crept back.

The main institutional response to the empire's problem was a progressive regimentation of its citizens. In part, this was in the tradition of regulating the economy which he

This 16th-century fresco is one of the few surviving representations of a session of the Church Council. The painting depicts the emperor at the Council of Ephesus in 431. He is banishing Nestor, patriarch of Constantinople, and another heretic.

had inherited. Just as peasants were tied to the soil, craftsmen were now attached to their hereditary corporations and guilds; even the bureaucracy tended to become hereditary. The resulting rigidity was unlikely to make imperial problems easier to solve.

RELIGION IN THE EASTERN EMPIRE

It was unfortunate that a quite exceptionally disastrous series of natural calamities fell on the East at the beginning of the sixth century: they go far to explain why it was hard for Justinian to leave the empire in better fettle than he found it. Earthquake, famine and plague devastated the cities and even the capital itself, where people saw phantoms in the

streets. The ancient world was a credulous place, but tales of the emperor's capacity to take off his head and then put it on again, or to disappear from sight at will, already suggest that under these strains the mental world of the Eastern Empire was already slipping its moorings in classical civilization. Justinian was to make the separation easier by his religious outlook and policies, another paradoxical outcome, for it was far from what he intended. After it had survived for eight hundred years, he abolished the academy of Athens; he wanted to be a Christian emperor, not a ruler of unbelievers, and decreed the destruction of all pagan statues in the capital. Worse still, he accelerated the demotion of the Jews in civic status and the reduction of their freedom to exercise their religion. Things had already gone a long way by then. Pogroms had long been connived at and synagogues destroyed; now Justinian went on to alter the Jewish calendar and interfere with the Jewish order of worship. He even encouraged barbarian rulers to persecute Jews. Long before the cities of western Europe, Constantinople had a ghetto.

Justinian was all the more confident of the rightness of asserting imperial authority in ecclesiastical affairs because (like the later James I of England) he had a real taste for theological disputation. Sometimes the consequences were unfortunate; such an attitude did nothing to renew the loyalty to the empire of the Nestorians and Monophysites, heretics who had refused to accept the definitions of the precise relationship of God the Father to God the Son laid down in 451 at a council at Chalcedon. The theology of such deviants mattered less than the fact that their symbolic tenets were increasingly identified with important linguistic and cultural groups. The empire began to create its Ulsters. Harrying heretics intensified separatist feeling in parts of Egypt and Syria. In

In the upper part of this fresco from the Coptic convent of St Apollinaris in Bauit, Egypt, Christ is depicted blessing the world. In the lower part, the Virgin Mary is shown sitting on a throne with the infant Jesus in her arms, surrounded by the Apostles.

the former, the Coptic Church went its own way in opposition to Orthodoxy in the later fifth century, and the Syrian Monophysites followed, setting up a "Jacobite" church. Both were encouraged and sustained by the numerous and enthusiastic monks of those countries. Some of these sects and communities, too, had important connexions outside the empire, so that foreign policy was involved. The Nestorians found refuge in Persia, and, though not heretics, the Jews were especially influential beyond the frontiers; Jews in Iraq supported Persian attacks on the empire and Jewish Arab states in the Red Sea interfered with the trade routes to India when hostile measures were taken against Jews in the empire.

DIVERGENCE OF EAST AND WEST

Justinian's hopes of reuniting the Western and Eastern Churches were to be thwarted in spite of his zeal. A potential division between them had always existed because of the different cultural matrices in which each had been formed. The Western Church had never accepted the union of religious and secular authority which was the heart of the political theory of the Eastern Empire; the empire would pass away as others had done (and the Bible told) and it would be the Church which would prevail against the gates of hell. Now such doctrinal divergences became more important, and separation had been made more likely by the breakdown in the West. A Roman pope visited Justinian and the emperor spoke of Rome as the "source of priesthood", but in the end the two Christian communions were first to go their own ways and then violently to quarrel. Justinian's own view, that the emperor was supreme, even on matters of doctrine, fell victim to clerical intransigence on both sides.

This seems to imply (as do so many others of his acts) that Justinian's real achievement was not that which he sought and temporarily achieved, the re-establishment of the imperial unity, but a quite different one, the easing of the path towards the development of a new, Byzantine civilization. After him, Byzantium was a reality, even if not yet recognized. It was evolving away from the classical world towards a style clearly related to it, but

This plaque, which represents an Evangelist or an Apostle, is thought to originate from the 6th-century early Christian abbey of Mettlach in Egypt.

The Egyptian Copts, who became Monophysites, formed a strong cult within Eastern Christianity. This Egyptian painting on wood depicts the Coptic abbot, Menas, with Christ, and is thought to date from the 6th or 7th century.

independent of it. This was made easier by contemporary developments in both Eastern and Western culture, by now overwhelmingly a matter of new tendencies in the Church.

THE ROLE OF THE BISHOPS IN THE LATE CLASSICAL AGE

As often in later history, the Church and its leaders had not at first recognized or welcomed an opportunity in disaster. They identified themselves with what was collapsing and understandably so. The collapse of empire was for them the collapse of civilization; the Church in the West was, except for municipal authority in the impoverished towns, often the sole institutional survivor of *romanitas*. Her bishops were men with experience of administration, at least as likely as other local notables to be intellectually equipped to grapple with new problems. A semi-pagan population looked to them with superstitious awe and attributed to them near-magical power. In many places they were the last embodiment of authority left when imperial

The Bishoi Coptic Monastery is situated in Wadi-al-Natrun in Egypt.

armies went away and imperial administration crumbled and they were lettered men among a new unlettered ruling class which craved the assurance of sharing the classical heritage. Socially, they were often drawn from the leading provincial families; that meant that they were sometimes great aristocrats and proprietors with material resources to support their spiritual role. Naturally, new tasks were thrust upon them.

CHRISTIAN MONASTICISM

THE END OF THE CLASSICAL WORLD also saw two new institutions emerge in the Western Church which were to be lifelines in the dangerous rapids between a civilization which had collapsed and one yet to be born. The first was Christian monasticism, a phenomenon first appearing in the East. It was about 285 that a Copt, St Anthony, retired to a hermit's life in the Egyptian desert. His example was followed by others who watched, prayed and strove with demons or mortified the flesh by fasting and more dubious disciplines. Some of them drew together in communities. In the next century this new form of spirituality established itself in a communal form in the Levant and Syria. From there, the idea spread to the West, to the Mediterranean coast of France. In a crumbling society such as fifth-century Gaul the monastic ideal of undistracted worship and service to God in prayer, within the discipline of an ascetic rule, was attractive to many men and women of intellect and character. Through it they could assure personal salvation. The communities attracted many from among the well-born who sought a refuge from a changing world. Unfriendly critics who hankered after the old Roman ideal of service to the state condemned them for shirking their proper responsibilities to society by withdrawing from it. Nor did churchmen always welcome what they saw as the desertion of some of the most zealous among their congregations. Yet many of the greatest churchmen of the age were monks and the institution prospered. Landowners founded communities or endowed existing ones with lands. There were some scandals and no doubt many compromises of principle in grappling with patrons and men of power.

ST BENEDICT

One Italian monk, of whom we know little except his achievement and that he was believed to work miracles, found the state of monasticism shocking. This was St Benedict, one of the most influential men in the Church's history. In 529 he set up a monastery at Monte Cassino in central Italy, giving it a new rule which he had compiled by sifting and selecting among others available. It is a seminal document of Western Christianity and therefore of Western civilization. It directed the attention of the monk to the community, whose abbot was to have complete authority. The community's purpose was not merely to provide a hotbed for the cultivation or the salvation of individual souls but that it should worship and live as a whole. The individual monk was to contribute to its task in the framework of an ordered routine of worship, prayer and labour. From the individualism of traditional monasticism a new human instrument was forged; it was to be one of the main weapons in the armoury of the Church.

This mosaic, which is from the 5th-century Mausoleum of Costantina in Rome, shows Christ delivering the law to St Peter and St Paul.

St Benedict and the founding of his monastic Rule

St Benedict was born c.480, in Nursia, central Italy. After studying in Rome, he was attracted by the solitary lifestyle of hermits, who devoted themselves to prayer and penitence, following the example of the Desert Fathers. Benedict retired to a grotto near Subiaco in the Abruzzi foothills where, over the next three years, he became famous among the local people because of the miracles he performed. As his reputation spread, he was invited to become abbot of a nearby monastery. However, Benedict found this an unrewarding experience, and soon returned to his refuge in Subiaco, where his followers established 12 communities of 12 monks under his leadership.

Legend has it that a scheming local priest, jealous of Benedict's fame, forced him to flee Subiaco in 529 by inciting a group of women to attack his communities. Benedict moved to Monte Cassino, between Rome and Naples, and founded the monastery where he was to spend the rest of his life. It was there that he composed the 73 chapters of his Rule. After his death in 543, the monastery was razed by the Lombards, but the monks found refuge in Rome. They received strong papal support, particularly from Gregory I (later canonized), whose *Dialogues* (Book 2) is the only recognized source to provide the details of St Benedict's life (Gregory's information came from four of the saint's disciples).

St Benedict's character can only be discovered from his Rule. Although he insisted that his monks take vows of chastity, poverty and obedience and of absolute loyalty to the monastery where they had taken those vows, St Benedict was also moderate and paternal, allowing the monks warm clothing and adequate sleep. The Rule specifies precise times for services and prayer, yet makes special provisions for the treatment of the sick and elderly. The enduring success of the Benedictine Rule is no doubt due to this blend of practicality and spirituality.

St Benedict of Nursia, known as the father of Western monasticism, is depicted in this fresco from the Cluniac monastery in Subiaco, Italy. St Benedict's motto "Pray and work" still governs the daily life of every Benedictine monk.

St Benedict did not set his sights too high and this was one secret of his success; the Rule was within the powers of ordinary men who loved God and his monks did not need to multilate either body or spirit. Its success in estimating their need was demonstrated by its rapid spread. Benedictine monasteries quickly appeared everywhere in the West. They became the key sources of missionaries and teaching for the conversion of pagan England and Germany. In the West, only the Celtic Church at its fringe clung to the older, eremitical model of the monkish life.

THE EARLY PAPACY

BESIDES THE BENEDICTINE MONASTERIES, the Church's other new great support was the papacy. The prestige of St Peter's see and the legendary guardianship of the Apostle's bones always gave Rome a special place among the bishoprics of Christendom. It was the only one in the West to claim descent from one of the Apostles. But in principle she had little else to offer; the Western Church was a junior branch and it was in the Churches of Asia that the closest links with the apostolic age

Many Benedictine monks dedicated themselves to producing religious manuscripts. In this illuminated manuscript from a 15th-century collection of writings on St Benedict, four of the saint's disciples are depicted assisting Pope Gregory the Great (540–604) with the compilation of his *Dialogues* or *Lives of the Saints*.

could be asserted. Something more was required for the papacy to begin its rise to the splendid pre-eminence which was taken for granted by the medieval world.

To begin with there was the city. Rome had been seen for centuries as the capital of the world, and for much of the world that had been true. Its bishops were the business colleagues of Senate and emperor and the departure of the imperial court only left their eminence more obvious. The arrival in Italy of alien civil servants from the Eastern Empire whom the Italians disliked as much as they did the barbarians directed new attention to the papacy as the focus of Italian

St Gregory the Great (540–604) is shown dictating a manuscript to two scribes in this 9th-century illustration. Gregory was recognized as a Father of the Church, in the Latin tradition.

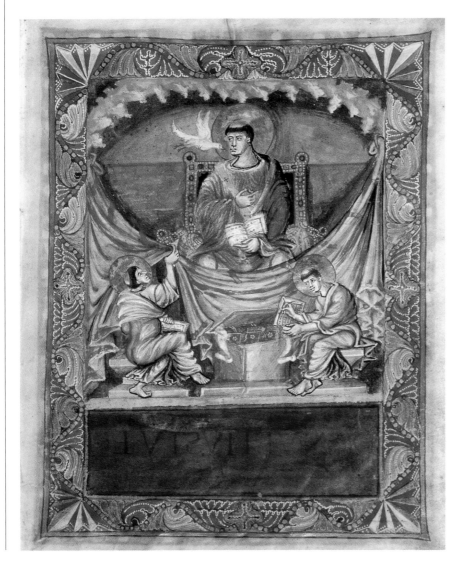

loyalties. It was, too, a wealthy see, with an apparatus of government commensurate with its possessions. It generated administrative skill superior to anything to be found outside the imperial administration itself. This distinction, too, stood out all the more clearly in times of trouble, when the barbarians lacked these skills. The see of Rome had the finest records of any; already in the fifth century papal apologists were exploiting them. The characteristically conservative papal stance, the argument that no new departures are being made but that old positions are being defended, is already present and was wholly sincere; popes did not see themselves as conquerors of new ideological and legal ground; but as men desperately trying to keep the small foothold the Church had already won.

This was the setting of the papacy's emergence as a great historical force. The fifth-century Leo the Great was the first pope under whom the new power of the bishop of Rome was clearly visible. An emperor declared papal decisions to have the force of law and Leo vigorously asserted the doctrine that the popes spoke in the name of St Peter. He assumed the title *pontifex maximus* discarded by the emperors. It was believed that his intervention by visiting Attila had staved off the Hun attack on Italy; bishops in the West who had hitherto resisted claims for Rome's primacy became more willing to accept them in a world turned upside-down by barbarians. Still, though, Rome was a part of the state church of an empire whose religion Justinian saw as above all the emperor's concern.

GREGORY THE GREAT

The pope in whom the future medieval papacy is most clearly revealed was also the first pope who had been a monk. In Gregory

This is the cover from a copy of the Gospels belonging to the Lombardian queen Theodelinda. It dates from 600 and was probably among the gifts sent to the queen by Pope Gregory the Great to thank her for helping to re-establish harmony between himself and her people. Theodelinda had used her influence to convince her husband and his subjects to renounce Arianism.

the Great, who reigned from 590 to 604, there thus came together the two great institutional innovations of the early Church. He was a statesman of great insight. A Roman aristocrat, loyal to the empire and respectful of the emperor, he was nevertheless the first pope who fully accepted the barbarian Europe in which he reigned; his pontificate at last reveals a complete break with the classical world. He saw as his duty the first great missionary campaign, one of whose targets was pagan England, to which he sent Augustine of Canterbury in 596. He struggled against the Arian heresy and was delighted by the conversion of the Visigoths to Catholicism. He was as much concerned with the Germanic kings as with the emperor in whose name he

claimed to act, but was also the doughtiest opponent of the Lombards; for help against them he turned both to the emperor and, more significantly, to the Franks. Yet the Lombards also made the pope, of necessity, a political power. Not only did they cut him off from the imperial representative at Ravenna but he had to negotiate with them when they stood before the walls of Rome. Like other bishops in the West who inherited civilian authority, he had to feed his city and govern it. Slowly Italians came to see the pope as successor to Rome as well as to St Peter.

AN EMERGING EUROPE

In Gregory the classical-Roman heritage and the Christian are subsumed; he represented something new though he can hardly have seen it like that. Christianity had been a part of the classical heritage, yet it was now turning away from much of it and was distinct from it. Significantly, Gregory did not speak Greek; nor did he feel he needed to. There had already been signs of transformation in the Church's relations with the barbarians. With Gregory, one focus of this story has come at last to be Europe, not the Mediterranean basin. There were already sown in it the seeds of the future, though not of the near future; for most of the world's people the existence of Europe for the next thousand years or so is almost irrelevant. But a Europe is at last discernible, unimaginably different though it may be from what was to come.

It was also decisively different from the past. The ordered, literate, unhurried life of the Roman provinces had given way to a fragmented society with, encamped in it, a warrior aristocracy and their tribesmen, sometimes integrated with the earlier inhabitants, sometimes not. Their chiefs were called

This votive crown, which belonged to the Visigoth king Recesvinto, dates from the second half of the 7th century. It is made of gold and precious stones and was found in the province of Toledo, Spain, along with other similar pieces that had been buried c.670.

kings and were certainly no longer merely chiefs, any more than their followers, after nearly two centuries of involvement with what Rome had left behind, were mere barbarians. It was in 550 that a barbarian king – a Goth – for the first time represented himself on his coins decked in the imperial insignia. Through the impression wrought on their imaginations by the relics of a higher culture, through the efficacy of the idea of Rome itself and through the conscious and unconscious work of the Church, above all, these peoples were on their way to civilization and their art remains to prove it.

THE MINGLING OF CHRISTIANITY AND PAGANISM

Of formal culture, the barbarians brought nothing with them to compare with antiquity. There was no barbarian contribution to the civilized intellect. Yet the cultural traffic was not all in one direction at less formal levels. The extent to which Christianity, or at least the Church, was still an elastic form must not be underestimated. Everywhere Christianity had to flow in the channels available and these were defined by layers of paganism, Germanic upon Roman upon Celtic. The conversion of a king like Clovis did not mean that his people made at once even a formal adherence to Christianity; some were still pagan after generations had passed, as their graves showed. But this conservatism presented opportunities as well as obstacles. The Church could utilize the belief in folk magic, or the presence of a holy site which could associate a saint with respect for age-old deities of countryside and forest. Miracles, knowledge of which was assiduously propagated in the saints' lives read aloud to pilgrims to their shrines, were the persuasive arguments of the age. People were used to the

magical interventions of the old Celtic deities or manifestations of Woden's power. For most men and women, for most of human history, the role of religion was not the provision of moral guidance or spiritual insight, but the propitiation of the unseen. Only over

The 7th-century Gospels from which this miniature is taken were produced at the Abbey of Durrow, in Ireland. The figure symbolizes St Matthew.

blood-sacrifice did Christianity draw the line between itself and the pagan past unambiguously; much other pagan practice and reminiscence it simply christened.

The process by which this came about has often been seen as one of decline and there are certainly reasonable arguments to be made to that effect. In material terms, barbarian Europe was an economically poorer place than the empire of the Antonines; all over Europe tourists gape still at the monuments of Rome's builders as our barbarian predecessors must have done. Yet out of this confusion something quite new and immeasurably more creative than Rome would emerge in due course. It was perhaps impossible for contemporaries to view what was happening in anything but apocalyptic terms. But some may have seen just a little beyond this, as the concerns of Gregory suggest.

From the manuscript of the *Homilies* of St Gregory, this miniature on parchment was produced in northern Italy in around 800. St Gregory, giving his blessing, sits beneath an arch adorned with geometric motifs and supported by two richly decorated columns.

Time chart (850 BCE–700 CE)

753 BCE
Legendary
foundation of Rome

| 800 BCE | 750 BCE | 700 BCE |

A golden tablet, which probably dates from
the early 5th century BCE, bearing Etruscan
and Phoenician inscriptions. The tablet forms
part of a treaty between Rome and Carthage,
confirming the relationship that had been
established when Rome was an Etruscan city.

Golden Etruscan tablet

Etruscan sculpture

The period 700–600 BCE saw
the height of the Etruscan
culture in central Italy. This
bronze Etruscan sculpture
represents a Chimaera – a
fire-breathing mythological
monster.

390 BCE
Defeat and sacki
Rome by the Gau

| 500 BCE | 450 BCE | 400 BCE |

509 BCE
Establishment of
the Roman Republic

493 BCE
Rome recognizes the
autonomy of the Latin cities

c.450 BCE
Law of the Twelve Tables

218–201 BCE
Second Punic
War

90–88 BCE
Social War: Roman
citizenship granted
to most of Italy

82–79 BCE
Sulla is dictator o
Roman Republic

| 200 BCE | 150 BCE | 100 BCE |

149–146 BCE
Third Punic War

106–43 BCE
Cicero, Roman orator

A bust of Publius Cornelius Scipio
236–184 BCE, who was known as
"Africanus" because of his
success in African campaigns
during the Second Punic War.

Publius Cornelius Scipio

Mithridates VI (132–63 BCE), king of
Pontus, tried to weaken the Roman
presence in Asia Minor and the
Aegean, but was defeated by Pompey.

Mithridates VI of Pontus

68–69 CE
Year of the
Four Emperors

96–192 CE
The adoptive emperors:
Nerva, Trajan, Adrian,
Antoninus Pius, Marcus
Aurelius and Commodus

117 CE
Trajan conquests: Empire
reaches maximum extent

193–235 CE
The Severus Dynasty, founded
by Septimius Severus

212 CE
Roman citizenship
granted to all Empire

| 100 CE | 150 CE | 200 CE |

66–70 CE
Jewish uprising
against Rome

The Roman city of Pompeii was buried
under volcanic ash from Mount Vesuvius
in 79 CE. This portrait of a married couple
was found in the city's ruins. The writing
boards and papyrus they are holding are
symbols of a good education.

Portrait of a Roman couple

The Roman Empire spread into Asia
Minor, where Roman culture merged
with local customs and beliefs. The keystone of the arch of Hadrian's Temple in
Ephesus, pictured here, bears an image
of the city's goddess.

Temple of Hadrian, Ephesus

379–395 CE
Reign of Emperor
Theodosius

| 400 CE | 450 CE | 500 CE |

395 CE
Final division of the
Roman Empire

419 CE
Visigoths found
kingdom of Toulouse

476 CE
Last Western Roman
emperor deposed

496 CE
Clovis converts to
Christianity

587 BCE
The Babylonians
conquer Jerusalem

650 BCE   600 BCE   550 BCE

Every property-owning male citizen
of the Roman Republic was obliged
to serve in the army. Conscription
lasted 16 years for an infantryman,
such as the one shown on this bone
tablet, and 10 for a cavalryman.

Roman soldier

343–290 BCE
Roman-Samnite wars:
Rome conquers central Italy

350 BCE   300 BCE   250 BCE

264–241 BCE
First Punic War

**Gaius Julius Caesar
(100–44 BCE)** came from a
well-known aristocratic
family and was the main
protagonist in the collapse
of the Roman Republic.

Bust of Julius Caesar

This marble statue of Octavianus Augustus,
who reigned as the first Roman emperor from
27 BCE–14 CE, portrays him as both a triumphant
general and a god – his bare feet symbolize his
divinity. At his side is Cupid on a dolphin,
respresenting Augustus' descent from Venus.

Roman emperor Augustus

71 BCE
Slave
revolt

58–50 BCE
Julius Caesar
in Gaul

44 BCE
Assassination
of Caesar

32–31 BCE
War of Octavian
against Antony
and Cleopatra

59 BCE–17 CE
Titus Livius, Roman historian

56–120 CE
Tacitus, Roman
historian

50 BCE   0   50 CE

70–19 BCE
Virgil,
oman poet

49–45 BCE
Civil War between
armies of Caesar
and Pompey

37–4 BCE
Reign of Herod the
Great, during which
Christ was born

26–36 CE
Pontius Pilate's government,
under which Christ died

Diocletian (284–305 CE),
established a tetrarchic
system. Two emperors ruled
(Diocletian in the East and
Maximian in the West) with
two *caesars*.

Diocletian and Maximian

Constantine the Great's reign as
Roman emperor (**306–337 CE**)
saw the reunification of the
empire under one ruler.

Emperor Constantine

330 CE
Foundation of
Constantinople

354–430 CE
St Augustine
of Hippo

250 CE   300 CE   350 CE

313 CE
Edict of Milan: tolerance
of Christian worship

This image of Christ, dated c.350 CE,
is from the St Ermite Roman catacomb.
His features are reminiscent of those in
Byzantine painting, which developed
in the Eastern Roman Empire.

Roman representation of Christ

Justinian, ruler of the Eastern
Roman Empire from **527–565 CE**,
codified Roman law and temporarily
reunited a large part of the old
Roman Empire.

Mosaic portrait of Justinian

590–604 CE
Gregory the Great
is Pope

550 CE   600 CE   650 CE

529 CE
St Benedict founds
western monastic Rule

587 CE
The Visigoth king Recared
converts to Catholicism

VOLUME 3 *Chapters and contents*

Chapter 1
Rome

The Etruscans 9
The Roman Republic 11
Early Republican government 12
The changing Republic 12
Oligarchy at work 14
Social foundations 15
The citizen class 15
The plebians 16
The constitution 17
The expansion of Roman power 17
The Punic Wars 18
Rome turns East 21
The growth of the Roman Empire 22
The imperial administration 24
Constitutional problems 25
Continuing Hellenization 25
Hellenistic influences 26
Stability 27
The decline of the Republic 27
Domestic crisis 27
Military service 28
Marius seizes power 30
Pompey 31
Julius Caesar 31
Caesar takes power 34
The end of the Republic 35

Chapter 2
The Roman Achievement

The Augustan Age 38
Augustus as consul 39
The benevolent despot 39
Monarchy and civil war 40
The Antonines 41
The limits of empire 41
Rome and Parthia 42
The *Pax Romana* 43
Imperial organization 46
Cosmopolitanism 47
Rome's Greek heritage 48
Law, engineering and town planning 51
Social divisions 55
Municipal life 57
Slavery 61
Religion 61
Religious cults 62
The imperial cult 63
External influences 65
Mystery cults 66
Unrest in the Empire 66
Taxation and the economy 68
The role of the army in the Roman state 69

Chapter 3
Jewry and the Coming of Christianity

The impact of Christianity 72
Christianity's Jewish origins 73
Jewish history 73
The Jews in exile 74
Independence and revolt 75
The spread of Judaism 76
The attractions of Judaism 77
The Jews under Roman rule 77
King Herod 79
Jewish unrest 79
Jesus of Nazareth 80
The Gospels' story of Jesus 80
Jesus' teaching 82
The followers of Christ 83
The teachings of St Paul 86
The spread of Christianity 87
Jewish extremists rebel 88
The dispersion 89
Hostility to Christianity 87
Persecution 91
The Church's survival 93
The Gnostics 94
The Fathers of the Church 95
The diffusion of Christianity in the classical
  world 96

Chapter 4

The Waning of the Classical West

Crisis and change 101
The last emperors' role 101
The importance of the army 101
Economic weakness 104
Inflation and increasing taxation 107
Confrontation with Parthia 107
The Persian threat 108
The European threat 111
The age of Diocletian 113
The Tetrarchy 114
The ideological crisis 114
The growth of the Christian Church 115
The persecution of Christians 117
Constantine the Great 118
Constantine and the Church 119
The Edict of Milan 120
Church and State 121
The Council of Nicaea 122
Christianity divided 123
Constantine's legacy 123

Disunity in the Empire 124
The decline of the West 127
The Germanic threat 129
The Visigoths 129
The growth of the Vandal Kingdom 133
The Huns 134
The collapse of the Western Empire 134
The barbarians' rise to power 134
The repression of paganism 136
The persecution of the Jews 137
Theodosius 137
The Christianization of the Empire 140
Rival religions 141
The life of St Augustine of Hippo 141
Augustine's spirituality 142
Baptism 143
Augustine and theology 144
Augustine's writings 144
The Two Cities 146
The legacy of St Augustine 148

Chapter 5

The Elements of a Future

The end of Romano-British civilization 150
The Franks 152
Clovis 153
The early Frankish nation 154
King Theodoric 154
Visigothic Spain 156
Roman and barbarian Western Europe 156
Germanic cultural legacy 158
The barbarians and the Roman tradition 158
Justinian 160
Justinian's legacy 164
Religion in the Eastern Empire 166
Divergence of East and West 168
The role of the bishops in the late
    classical age 169
Christian monasticism 170
St Benedict 171
The early papacy 173
Gregory the Great 174
An emerging Europe 176
The mingling of Christianity and paganism 177

SERIES CONTENTS

Volume 1

**PREHISTORY
AND THE FIRST
CIVILIZATIONS**

Before History
The Foundations
Homo sapiens
The Possibility of
 Civilization

The First Civilizations
Early Civilized Life
Ancient Mesopotamia
Ancient Egypt
Intruders and Invaders:
 the Dark Ages of the
 Ancient Near East

Volume 2

**EASTERN ASIA AND
CLASSICAL GREECE**

**The Beginnings of
Civilization in Eastern Asia**
Ancient India
Ancient China
The Other Worlds of
 the Ancient Past
The End of the Old World

**The Classical
Mediterranean: Greece**
The Roots of One World
The Greeks
Greek Civilization
The Hellenistic World

Volume 3

**ROME AND THE
CLASSICAL WEST**

Rome
The Roman Achievement
Jewry and the Coming
 of Christianity
The Waning of the
 Classical West
The Elements of a Future

Volume 4

**THE AGE OF
DIVERGING
TRADITIONS**

Islam and the Re-making
 of the Near East
The Arab Empires
Byzantium and its Sphere
The Disputed Legacies of
 the Near East
The Making of Europe

Volume 5

**THE FAR EAST AND
A NEW EUROPE**

India
Imperial China
Japan
Worlds Apart
Europe: the First
 Revolution
Europe Looks Outward

Volume 6

THE MAKING OF THE EUROPEAN AGE

A New Kind of Society: Early Modern Europe
Authority and its Challengers
The New World of Great Powers
Europe's Assault on the World
World History's New Shape

Volume 7

THE AGE OF REVOLUTION

Ideas Old and New
Long-term Change
Political Change in an Age of Revolution
A New Europe
The Anglo-Saxon World

Volume 8

THE EUROPEAN EMPIRES

The European World Hegemony
European Imperialism and Imperial Rule
Asia's Response to a Europeanizing World
Strains in the System
The Era of the First World War

Volume 9

EMERGING POWERS AND THE LATEST AGE

A New Asia in the Making
The Ottoman Heritage and the Western Islamic Lands
The Second World War
The Shaping of a New World
Population, Economy and the Management of Nature
Ideas, Attitudes and Authority

Volume 10

THE NEW WORLD ORDER

The Politics of the New World
Inheritors of Empire
Crumbling Certainties
New Challenges to the Cold War World Order
The End of an Era
Epilogue: in the Light of History

INDEX

Page references to main text in roman, to box text in **bold** and to captions in *italic*.

A

Abgar VIII (or IX), Christian king of Osrhoene 72
Achaemenid Empire 108–9
Africa
  Christianity in 141–2, 144
  as the granary of the Roman Empire 127, *133*
  as a Roman province 126
  secure frontiers of 107
  capture of by Vandals 133
Agilulf, king of the Lombards (590–616 CE) *161*
agriculture
  the Roman economy and 15, 69, 104–7
  self-supporting estates and 128
  smallholdings and 28, 29
Agrippa, Marcus Julius, "Herod", (10 BCE–44 CE), Jewish king of Palestine 90
Agrippa, Marcus Vipsanius (63–12 BCE), Roman general *40*, 53
Alamanni 129
  invasion of Rome by 111
  defeat of by Franks 153
Alans, nomadic pastoral people 132, 133
Alexandria
  Jewish colony of 77
  unrest in 68, 77
Ambrose, St (c.340–397 CE), bishop of Milan 137–40, *141*
Anatolia, ravaged by Huns 134
Angles, Germanic peoples 150
Anglo-Saxon kingdoms 150
Antiochus IV, king of Syria (175–164 BCE) 75, *75*
Antoninus Pius (86–161 CE), Roman emperor (136–161 CE) 41
Antony, St (c.250–350 CE), Christian hermit 170, *172*
Apollonius of Tyana (1st century CE), Greek philosopher 66
Appian Way 47
Arcadius, Flavius, Eastern Roman emperor (383–408 CE) *134*
Archimedes (c.287–212 BCE), Greek mathematician 26
architecture *62*, *143*, *164*
  Roman technical skills 51–5, **52**, *53*
  water supply infrastructure **59**
  see also Byzantine Empire, architecture
Ardashir I (Artaxerxes), king of Persia (224–240 CE) 108, **109**, *111*
Arian Baptistry, Ravenna *122*, *123*
Arianism, Christian heresy 122–3, *123*, 176
  Germanic peoples and 141, *155*, *157*, *159*
Arius (c.260–336 CE), Christian heretic 122–3, *123*
  Athanasius' opposition to 123
Armenia, kingdom between Rome and Parthia 42, *43*, 108, 110
  Persian conquest of 109, **109**
Arminius (17 BCE–21 CE), German chieftain 42
art
  Byzantine **163**

Etruscan *8*, *10*, *11*
Greek *13*, 26
Ludovisi sarcophagus bas-reliefs *130*
see also frescoes; jewellery; mosaics; sculpture
Arthur (6th century CE), legendary Romano-British king 150
Asia Minor
  Christianity in 126
  Roman forces in 22
Athalaric, Ostrogoth king (526–534 CE) *158*
Athanasius (c.295–373 CE), bishop of Alexandria 123
Athens, as part of Roman Empire 22
Attila (c.406–453 CE), king of the Huns (434–453 CE) 134
  Leo the Great and 174
Augustine, St, archbishop of Canterbury (601–604 CE) 176
  missionary campaign of 176
Augustine, St (354–430 CE), bishop of Hippo (396–430 CE) 141–8, *149*, *174*
  baptism of by St Ambrose 143, *145*
  The City of God and 144–7, *145*, 148, *149*
  Donatists and 143, 144, 148
  puritanism and 144
  influence of on medieval political thought 144
  Manichaeism and 143
Augustus (Gaius Julius Caesar Octavianus) (63 BCE–14 CE), first Roman emperor (27 BCE–14 CE) 6, *39*, 40, 42, 62, *71*
  administrative reforms under 46–7
  deification of 40
  pontifex maximus and 39, 63, 174
  republican forms maintained under 39, 101
  rise to power of 38–40
  statesmanship of **42**
  successors of 40
Aurelian (Lucius Domitius Aurelianus) (c.215–275 CE), Roman emperor (270–275 CE) *107*, 113
Aurelius Antoninus, Marcus (121–180 CE), Roman emperor (161–180 CE) **33**, 41, *41*
Australasia 152, 154

B

Babylon
  Solomon's temple at 73
  Persian overthrow of 75
Bar Kochba, Simon (2nd century CE), Jewish messianic claimant 90
barbarians
  assimilation into Europe of **126**, 129, 132, 134–5
  civilizing influences acting upon 176–7
  cultural legacy of 158
  imperial army employment of **126**, 129, 132, 134–5
  Gaul threatened by 30
  migrations of **126**, 129, 132, 133
  tribes of 132, 134–5, 153
  tribute paid to 107
  Western Empire overcome by 127–136

see also individual names of tribes
Bath, thermal springs at 151, *151*
battles **20**
  Actium (31 BCE) 38
  Adrianople (378 CE) 132
  Cannae (216 BCE) 19
  Lake Trasimene (217 BCE) 19
  Zama (202 BCE) 19–21, 22
Bede (c.673–735 CE), English scholar and monk 154
Belgium, Frankish settlement of 152, 153
Belisarius (c.506–65 CE), Roman general 161
Benedict of Nursia, St (c.480–c.544 CE), monasticist 171–3, *172*
Benedictine Rule **172**
Boadicea (d.62 CE), queen of the Iceni 68
Boethius, Anicius Manlius Severinus (c.480–524 CE), Roman philosopher 155, *155*
Boscoreale villa *see* Pompeii; frescoes
Britain
  Celtic peoples of 150
  Claudius's conquest of 42
  Germanic invasions of 150–52
  Hadrian's Wall 42, *43*, 125, 151
  reconnaissance of by Caesar 42
Brutus, Marcus Junius (c.85–42 BCE), Roman aristocrat 12
Burgundians, Germanic peoples 129
  defeat of by Franks **152**, 153
Byzantine Empire, the **163**
  architecture of *163*, *164*
  art of **163**
  expansion of under Justinian **160**
  naval power of 163
  sale of offices in 165
  see also Roman Empire
Byzantium, capital of the Eastern Empire **119**, 168

C

Caesar, Gaius Julius (c.102–44 BCE), Roman general and dictator 6, 31–6, *34*, *36*, *37*, *44*
  assassination of 35, 38
  Britain and 41–2
  The Conquest of Gaul **32**
  deification of 36, 40
  dictatorship of 34
  Gaul and 31–2, *32*, 42
  Octavian and 38
  Pompey defeated by 34
  Rubicon, crossing of the 32
calendar, Julian 35
Callimachus, Greek sculptor 26
Cappadocia 118
Caracalla (Marcus Aurelius Antoninus, "Caracallus") (186–217 CE), Roman emperor (211–217 CE) 103, *103*, 104, *104*
Carthage *128*
  destruction of by Scipio Aemilianus 19, **20**, 23
  new city of *19*
  Pyrrhus, campaigns of 18

religious rituals at 142
  in Second Punic War 19
  capture of by Vandals 133
  treaty between Rome and 10
catacombs
  of Domitilla (Rome) *85*
  of St Ermite (Rome) *100*
  in Naples 96
  of Priscilla (Rome) *77*, *89*, *94*
  of Via Latina (Rome) *74*
cataphracts, Parthian heavy cavalry 42
Cato, Marcus (234–149 BCE), Roman statesman 22
Celtic Church 173
Celtic peoples
  location in Britain of 150
  incursions into Gaul of 27
  Romano-British Christianity preserved by 152
Chalcedon, Council of 166
chariot races *60*, 60
Childeric I, Merovingian king (460–481 CE) *129*
Chlotar I, king of the Franks (511–561 CE) *153*
Christianity 6, 12, **91**
  in Africa 141–3
  in Asia Minor 126
  Augustine and 144–8
  Constantine and 122
  doctrinal divergences of 166–7, 168
  in East and West 140, 143, 168–9
  in the Eastern Empire 166–8
  Europe, impact of 72
  Greek philosophy and 116–17, 123
  heresy and 141, 166–7, *166*
  hierarchical structure of Church in 88, **91**
  Jewish origins of 73–80
  Judaism, influence on 77
  Julian the Apostate and 135–6
  martyrdom in 85, 90–91, *92*, *94*
  missionary activity in **88**, 115, 118, 140, **172**
  mystery cults and 66
  origin and development of 80–78
  orthodox Judaism and 87
  pagan rites assimilated into 177–8
  as a philosophy 95
  Roman reaction to 87, 91, 115–18
  spread of 87–8, **91**, 99, 115, 118
  see also religions; Roman Catholic Church; Roman religions
Christianity, conversions to
  Abgar, king of Osrhoene 72
  Augustine, St 143, *145*
  Clovis, king of the Franks **152**, 153, **157**, 177
  Constantine 120–22
  Paul, St 86, *116*
  Visigoths **157**
Christians
  diaspora (dispersion) 76, 90, 95
  persecution of 90–93, *91*, *92*, 117–18
  property of, restored under Edict of Milan 120–21
Church Councils
  Chalcedon 166
  Ephesus 166

Nicaea 122–3, *123*, 141
Church and state
    conflict between, in West **125**, 126–7, 140
    linking of by Constantine 124, **125**, 143
churches
    Arian baptistry (Ravenna) *122, 123*
    in Dura Europos *121*
    Neonian baptistry (Ravenna) *81*
    St Apollinaris basilica of Classe
        (Ravenna) *159, 163*
    Sts Cosmas and Damian (Rome) *72*
    Santa Costanza (Rome) *85*
    San Lorenzo (Milan) *143*
    San Pedro de la Nave (Zamora) *157*
    St Peter (Rome) *86*
    St Simeon basilica, Qalaat Semaan *115*
    St Sofia (Constantinople) *163*, 164, *164*
    San Vitale (Ravenna) *146, 159, 161*
Cicero, Marcus Tullius (106–43 BCE),
    Roman orator *28*, 62, 143
citizenship, Roman
    army service and 29, **33**
    decline in influence of 16
    extension of to allies and subjects 16, 28, 30, 47
    in the republic 14, 15–16, 28
The City of God (St Augustine) 144–7, *145*,
    148, *149*
Claudius (Tiberius Claudius Nero)
    (10 BCE–54 CE), Roman emperor (41–54 CE)
    42, 54, 64
Clement of Alexandria, St (1st century CE),
    Christian Platonist 96, 117
Cleopatra (c.68–30 BCE), queen of Egypt
    (51–30 BCE) 34, 38, *38*
Clovis (465–511 CE), king of the Franks
    (481–511 CE) **152**, 153–4, 156, **157**, 158
Codex Constitutionum 54
coinage *38*
    debased in late Roman Empire 107
    Parthian 108
Commodus, Lucius Aelius Aurelius
    (161–192 CE), Roman emperor (180–192 CE)
    41, 101, *102*
Constantine I (Flavius Valerius Constantinus)
    (c.285–337 CE), Roman emperor (306–337 CE)
    118–24, *118*, **119**, *120, 121, 123*
    Caesaropapism 121
    conversion of to Christianity 119–21, 122, 123
    Council of Nicaea and 122, *123*
    foundation of Constantinople by 124
    tax reforms and 119
Constantinople *119*, 119, 124, 137, 160–61, **163**
Constantius, Flavius Valerius (c.225–300 CE),
    Roman emperor in West (305–306 CE) 118
consuls 14, 16, 25, 34, 39
    Augustus 39
    Caesar 31
    Marius 29
Coptic Church *142, 167*, 168, *169*, 170, *170*
Crassus, Marcus Licinius (c.108–53 BCE),
    Roman politician 42, 43, *44*
Ctesiphon, capital of Parthia
    conquest of by Ardashir I 108
    conquest of by Trajan 43
Cyprus, annexation of by Rome 27

D

Dacia, Roman province
    abandonment of 112
    conquest of by Trajan 42, *44*
    gold mines of 69

Danube, the
    barbarian threat to 110, 129
    as frontier of empire 42, 125
    Goths and 111
    Visigoths and 132
Dead Sea Scrolls (Qumran writings) 80, *80*, 81
Decius, Gaius Nessius Quintus (201–251 CE),
    Roman emperor (249–251 CE)
    murder of by Goths 118
    persecution of Christians by 117
Diocletian (Gaius Aurelius Valerius Diocletianus)
    (245–316 CE), Roman emperor (284–305 CE)
    14, 113–15, *114*
    persecution of Christians by 118
divination
    by interpretation of omens *10*
    Oracle of Fortuna Primigenia *21*
    by reading of auguries 12
Domitian (Titus Flavius Domitianus) (51–96 CE),
    Roman emperor (81–96 CE) 41
    residence of on Palatine Hill *45*
Donatists, Christian schismatics 121, 141
    Augustine's attacks on 143, 144, 148
Dura-Europos *121*
    synagogue of *73*
    temple of Palmyran gods in *75*

E

economic developments 68–9, *70*
    agricultural base of 15, 69, 104–7
    fiscal policies 46, 104–7, 114, 119, 165–6
    inflation 107, 135
    restoration of money economy 119
    tax base 106, 114, 127–8, 133, 135
    trade 69, *70*, 109–10, **109**, 128
    wage and price freeze 114
    weaknesses of 104–7
Edict of Milan 120–21
Egypt
    annexation of by Rome 38–9
    Christianity in 123, 126, 166–7, *168*
    Coptic Church in *142, 167*, 169, 170
    Julius Caesar and Cleopatra and 34
    Monophysites *169*
    Ptolemaic state ends in 38
Emporiae, Greek city *23*
engineering, Roman **52**
entertainments, public 58–9, 60, *60*, *92, 94*, 137
Ephesus, Council of 166
Epicureanism 51
Epigrams (Martial) 58
Essenes, Jewish sect *80*
Etruscans 8, 9–11, *10, 11*
    Latin cities revolt against 12
    lifestyle and beliefs of **10**
Euphrates, frontier of Roman Empire 42, 43
Europe 112
    barbarian influences on 156–60
    Christianity, impact of in 72
    increasing importance of 176
    roots in Germanic invasions 150
Ezekiel (7th century BCE), Hebrew prophet 73
Ezra (mid-5th century BCE), Hebrew
    prophet *75*

F

Fall of the Roman Republic (Plutarch) 31
foederati 132, 134–5, 153
France *see* Gaul

Franks, the 129, 152–6, 176
    in Belgium *152*, 153
    Clovis, king of **152**, 153–4, 156, **157**, 158
    as *foederati* 153
    growth of kingdom of the **152**
    invasion of Rome by 111
    kingdom of split into parts 154
    see also Germanic peoples; Goths; Ostrogoths;
        Visigoths
frescoes *57, 73, 75, 166, 167*
    Boscoreale villa *51, 56, 105, 106*
Frisians (Germanic peoples) 129

G

Galerius Valerius Maximianus, Gaius
    (c.250–311 CE), Roman emperor (305–311 CE)
    118, *124*
Gaul
    barbarian invasions of 111, 132–4, 152
    defeat of by Caesar 32, 42
    establishment of a Frankish kingdom at Tournai
        152, 153, 154
    as a Roman province 27
    Toulouse, Visigoth kingdom of 132–3,
        156, **157**, 158
generals
    Belisarius 161
    Caesar Augustus *see* Augustus
    Hannibal 19–20, 28
    Julius Caesar *see* Caesar
    Mark Antony 21, 38, *38*, 43
    political role of 25
    Pompey 31, *31*, 34, 37, 76
    Stilicho 134
    Sulla 30–31, *32*, 42, 146
Germania, The (Tacitus) **132**
Germanic peoples, the 129–33, *132*, **132**
    Angles 150
    blood feuds of 158
    Burgundians 129, **152**, 153
    division of by Rhine 46
    Franks *see* Franks
    Frisians 129
    Jutes 150
    legions defeated by 42
    Lombards *see* Lombards
    migrations of the **126**, 129, 132, 133, **160**
    movements into Britain of 150–52
    Ostrogoths *see* Ostrogoths
    Saxons 129, 150
    as a threat to northern frontier **33**, 110–12
    Thuringians 129
    Vandals *see* Vandals
    Visigoths *see* Visigoths
Germanicus Julius Caesar (15 BCE–19 CE),
    Roman general 39
Geta, Lucius Septimius, brother of
    Caracalla *103*
gladiatorial games and wild-beast shows 12
    brutality of 58–9, 60, *92, 94*
Gnosticism, Christian heresy 94–5, 96, 141
Goths
    in Crimea 164
    invasion of Moesia and Greece by 111
    see also Franks; Germanic peoples; Ostrogoths;
        Visigoths
government and administration
    in the republic 12–17, 24–5
    in the Roman Empire
        Constantine reform 119
        decline 127–8, 135

imperial bureaucracy 39–40, 46–7,
    101–103, 113
    Justinian reform 164–6
    reorganization under Diocletian 113–14,
        118
governors, provincial 24–5
Gracchus, Gaius (153–121 BCE), brother of
    Tiberius Gracchus 29
Gracchus, Tiberius (163–133 BCE), Roman
    agrarian reformer 29, 30
Greek influences on Rome 13, 26–7, 48–51, *50*
Gregory I, "the Great" (c.540–604 CE), Pope
    (590–604 CE) *173*, 174–6, *174, 175*
Gregory, St (538–594 CE), bishop of Tours 154

H

Hadrian (Publius Aelius Hadrianus)
    (76–138 CE), Roman emperor (117–138 CE)
    41, 43, *43, 53*, 68, 90
Hadrian's Wall 42, *43*, 125, 151
Hannibal (247–182 BCE), Carthaginian general
    19–20, *28*
Herod the Great (74–4 BCE), king of Judaea
    (40–4 BCE) 79, *79*
    Temple rebuilding begun by 78
Herodium 79
Histories, The (Tacitus) **41**
History of the Franks (Gregory) 154
Honorius, Flavius (384–423 CE), Western Roman
    emperor (395–423 CE) 134
Huns, Asian nomads
    Attila and Leo the Great 174
    defeat of by Visigoth army 134, 152
    Goths and *126*, 132

I

Irenaeus (c.130–202 CE), bishop of Lyons 95–6
iron, in Elba 11
Isis, Egyptian goddess 68, *93*
Islam, expansion of **160**, 164

J

James (later St), apostle of Jesus 85
Jerome, St (c.340–420 CE), Christian churchman
    148, *174*
Jerusalem *78*, 78
    Antonia fortress *78*
    Christ's entry into 81–2, *83*
    conquest of by Babylon 73
    Hadrian and 90
    sacking of by Romans (70 CE) 88
    see also Solomon's Temple
Jesus of Nazareth (c.4 BCE–29/30 CE) 68, 72, *84,
    85, 100*, 117, 138
    baptism of by John 81, *81*, 122
    disciples of (Apostles) 82, 83, *84*, 85, *85*, 122
    entry into Jerusalem of 81–2, *83*
    Jewish reactions to teachings of 82–5
    life of 80–82
    resurrection of 82, 85, **87**, 89, **91**, 96
    teachings of 82–3, *82*
    trial and crucifixion of 82
jewellery *124, 132, 154, 156, 176*
    Gemma augustae *39*
Jews
    civic status of under Justinian 166
    covenant with God 73, *76*

diaspora (dispersion) **76**, 90, 95
dislike of by Roman populace 77
divisions between 79–80
Exile of 73, 74–5
Hellenization of 75, 76
Judean War against Rome (66–74 CE) **78**, 89
legal status of 90, 166
Maccabaean revolt and (168–164 BCE) 75, *75*
Messiah, prophesied by the 80, 82, 83, 85
as Persian allies 168
persecution of by Christian emperors 137, 166
resistance to Rome of 68
Roman rule and 77–80
spiritual nationalism of under Rome 47–8, 68, **76**, 80, 89–90
theocratic view of history of 73, 77
John the Baptist (1st century BCE), prophet 81, *81, 122, 146*
Josephus, Flavius (37–c.100 CE), Jewish historian 89
Judaea 76, 79, 80, 88
conquest of by Titus 69
Jewish rebellion in 89
Simon bar Kochba and 90
Judah, Hebrew kingdom of 74, 75
independence of 76
punishment of 73
Judaism
attractions of 77
beliefs of **76**
development of synagogues 74
established orthodoxy of 101
Law of Moses (Mosaic Law) 73, 74, 75, **76**, 83, 89
Christianity and 87, **91**
Pharisaic reformation of 76
proselytism of 76, 77, 137
shaped by Exile 74
as source of Christianity 73
spread of 76–7
Julian calendar 35
Julian "the Apostate" (Flavius Claudius Julianus) (332–363 CE), Roman emperor (361–363 CE) 135–6, *135*
Justin Martyr (c.100–c.163 CE), Christian churchman 117
Justinian I (483–562 CE), Roman emperor in East (527–562 CE) 157, 160–69, *161, 162*
administrative reforms of 165–6
Athens Academy closed by 166
building programme of *159, 162*, 163, **163**, 164, *165*
capture of Ravenna by 159
Codex Constitutionum of **54**
ecclesiastical supremacy and 166, 168, 174
extent of empire of **160**
failure of in uniting Western and Eastern Churches by 168–9
Jutes, Germanic peoples 150

K

Kochba, Simon bar (2nd century CE), Jewish messianic claimant 90

L

languages 126
Greek 48, 77
Latin 48, **50**, 156, 160

Latin people 12
law and legal institutions
blood feuds 158
Germanic codifications 158
Mosaic Law 73, 74, 75, **76**, 83, 89
Roman 27, 51, **54**
codification of by Justinian *162*, 164
Romano-Visigoth code **157**
Leo I, "the Great" (c.390–461 CE), Pope (440–461 CE) 174
Lepcis Magna, Africa *104*
Levant, communal monasticism in the 170
literacy
in the army 48
among the Etruscans 11
in barbarian kingdoms 158
Livy (Titus Livius) (59 BCE–17 CE), Roman historian 51, 62
Lombards, Germanic peoples 129, 156, *161*, *163*, 175
Gregory the Great's opposition to 176

M

Macedon 21, 26
as a Roman province 22
Manichaeism, Christian heresy 141
in Africa 143
maps
Punic Wars **20**
Imperial residences on Palatine Hill **45**
Jerusalem *78*
Judaism of the ancient world **69**
Justinian's empire 527–565 CE **160**
Migrations of Germanic peoples **126**
Roman Empire, expansion of **35**
Roman Empire, two parts **125**
Roman roads **55**
St Paul's journeys **88**
Sassanid Empire in 4th century CE **109**
Southern Italy 509–272 BCE **9**
Marius, Gaius (155–186 BCE), Roman general and consul 29, 30, 31, *146*
Mark Antony (83–30 BCE), Roman general
Cleopatra and 38, *38*
defeat of by Parthians 43
marriage
between Romans and barbarians 156
martyrdom, Christian 85, 90–91, *92, 94*
Masada 89
Martial (Marcus Valerius Martialis) (c.40–c.104 CE), Roman writer 58
mausoleums
of Constantina (Rome) *120, 171*
of Ravenna *138, 156*
Maximian (Marcus Aurelius Valerius Maximianus) (c.240–310 CE), Roman co-emperor (285–305 CE) 113
Maximinus, Gaius Julius Verus, Roman emperor (235–238 CE) 103
Merovingian Dynasty 152, *153*, 154
relocation of capital in Paris 152, *154*
Childeric I, king *129*
see also Franks
Mesopotamia 108, *109*
metallurgy, Etruscan *8*, 11
Mildenhall Treasure *24*
military developments
elephants and 19, *28*
Parthian cavalry 42
Roman infantry 18
Mithraism 65, 66, 67, **68**, 93, *121*

Mithridates VI (132–63 BCE), king of Pontus (120–63 BCE) 27, *31*
monastic life **172**
monasticism, Christian 170–73, **172**
Monophysites, Christian heretics 166, 168, *169*
monuments, Roman **52**
Ara Pacis Augustae *40*
archway, city of Glanum *23*
funerary *29, 156*
to Gelio Publicola, censor *24*
to Marcus Aurelius *41*
to Mark Antony *21*
Trajan's column *44*
triumphal arch, Arausio *34*
mosaics *138, 140, 171*
Byzantine *161, 162*, **163**
Roman *16*, 60, *92*, 138, *140*
depicting Ambrose, St *141*
depicting Christ *72, 81*, 85, *122, 171*
in North Africa *49, 50, 128*
depicting Paul, St *86, 116*
Moses (c.13th century BCE), Hebrew patriarch 74, *74*, 76
Muslims
arrival in Spain **157**
Islamic expansion **160**, 164

N

neo-Platonism 51
Nero Claudius Caesar (37–68 CE), Roman emperor (54–68 CE) 40
persecution of Christians by 87, 90, *91*
Nerva (Marcus Cocceius Nerva) (c.35–98 CE), Roman emperor (96–98 CE) 41
Nestorians, Christian heretics 166, *166*, 168
Neustria 154
conquest of by Franks 152
New Testament
Acts of the Apostles 83, 87, **88**, 90
Gospel record of Jesus 80–82, **91**
Nicaea, Council of 122–3, *123*, 141

O

Octavian *see* Augustus
Odoacer (d.493 CE), German chieftain 134, *147*, 160
Old Testament 74, **76**, 77, 83, **91**
Origen (c.185–c.254 CE), Christian theologian 96, 117
Osrhoene, Syrian kingdom 72
Ostrogoths, Germanic peoples 129, 132, 154–6, *156*
Arianism 155
Athalaric, king of the *158*
eviction of from Rome 161
loss of Ravenna to Justinian 159
Theodoric, king of the 154–6, *156*, *158*, 160
see also barbarians; Goths; Visigoths
Ovid (Publius Ovidius Naso) (43 BCE–17 CE), Roman poet 40

P

Palmyra *108*
Roman alliance with 112
Pantheon (Rome) *53*, 68

Papacy, the 173–6
administrative skills of 174
Pope Gregory I 174–6
Pope Leo I 174
Paris, as Merovingian capital 152, *154*
Parthia
cataphracts (heavy cavalry), use of in 42
conflict between Rome and 107–8, *110*
Ctesiphon, capital city of 43, 108
Roman forces of 42, 43, *44*
Paul of Tarsus (later St), Christian apostle 85, 86, *86*, 90–91, 117
journeys of 87, **88**
letters of 87
missionary teachings of 87, **88**, **91**, *116*
Pax Romana 43–6, 69
peasants 29, 106, 114
Pelagianism, Christian heresy 141
Augustine's opposition to 144
Pentateuch 74
Pergamon, kingdom of 22, 27
Persia 112, 125
invasion of Syria by 109, **109**
Justinian and 160, 161, 164
Sassanid Dynasty 108–9, *111*
trade in 109–10, **109**
Peter (later St), apostle of Jesus 85, *85*, 90–91
confers status on bishopric of Rome 173
Pharisees 76, 80, 82, 83, 85
Pilate (Pontius Pilatus), Roman governor of Judaea (26–36 CE) 79, 89
Plato (c.427–c.347 BCE), Greek philosopher, influence on Christianity 96, 117
Pliny the Younger (62–113 CE), Roman administrator 57
Plutarch (Lucius Mestrius Plutarchus) (c.50–c.120 CE), Roman biographer 31
political systems
autocracy (Justinian) 161, 164
benevolent despotism (Rome) 39–40
despotic monarchy (Rome) 101
dictatorship (Rome) 30, *32*
divine kingship (Rome) 63–5, 113–15
oligarchy (Rome) 14–17, 31
satrapy (Persia) 47
tetrarchy (Rome)114–15
theocratic satrapy (Judah) 75
Polybius (c.201–120 BCE), Roman historian 26–7
Pompeii *17*, 57, *58*, 67
Boscoreale villa *51, 56, 105, 106*
Pompey (Gnaeus Pompeius Magnus) (106–46 BCE), Roman general 31, *31, 37*, *44*, 76
defeat of by Caesar 34
Popes
Gregory I *173*, 174–6, *174*
Leo I 174
Postumus, Marcus Cassianius Latinius (d.267 CE), emperor in Gaul 103
Praxiteles (4th century BCE), Greek sculptor 13
Probus Orestes, Rufus Genadius, Roman consul 158
Punic Wars 18–23, *19*, **20**, *23*, 28, *28*
Pyrrhus (c.318–272 BCE), king of Epirus (295–272 BCE) 18, *19*, *28*

Q

quaestors 14–15
Qumran 80, *80, 81*

R

Radegunda, Queen, wife of Chlotar I *153*
Ravenna 135, *146*, **163**, 176
  Justinian and *159*
  mosaics of *81, 138, 161, 163*
  Theodoric and 154, *156*, 160
Recared I, king of Visigoths (586–601 CE) **157**
Recesvinto, king of the Visigoths (653–672 CE) *176*
religions
  in Eastern Empire 166–8
  Etruscan *10*
  Mithraism 65, 66, 67, **68**, 93, *121*
  mystery cults 66, 67, **68**, 93–5
  see also Christianity; Roman religion
Rhine, the
  barbarian threat to 110, 129
  crossing of by Vandals and Alans 133
  Franks and 111
  as frontier of empire 42, 125
Roman army, the 9, 17–18, *18*, *33*, 69–70
  barbarian mercenaries **126**, 129, 132, 134–5
  basis of power of 40, 70
  citizenship earned by service in 29, *33*
  conscription into 17–18, 28–9, *33*, 114
  construction labour, as source of 51–4
  declining effectiveness of 128–9
  defeat of by Germanic tribes 42
  defeat of by Parthians 42, 43
  entry of into politics 29
  growth of in later empire 107–8, 114
  Herod's Temple, destruction of by **78**
  legionary standards in 29, 43
  military camps in 59, **111**
  Mithraism 65, 66
  new emperors chosen by 41, 70, 101, 113
  Praetorian Guard 33, 38, 70, *71*, 101
    disbanded by Constantine 119
  property qualifications abolished in 29, **33**
  reorganization of
    under Aurelian 112–13
    under Constantine 119
    under Diocletian 114
  soldiers' pay in 107, *107*
  strength of 33, 70
  tetrarchy and 114
  veterans of *34, 39*
  volunteers in 70
Roman Catholic Church, the
  St Augustine baptized in 143
  bishops, role of in 169–70, 174
  conversions to
    Clovis, king of the Franks **152**, *153*
    Recared, king of the Visigoths **157**
    Visigoths in Spain 156, **157**, 176
  Donatists and 143
  missionary campaigns of 176
  Arian barbarians and 141
  political importance of 153
  rise of Papacy in 173–4
  see also Papacy
Roman citizenship
  army service and 29, **33**
  decline in influence of 16
  extension of 16, 28, 30, 47
  in republic 14, 15–16, 28
Roman emperors
  Antoninus Pius (136–161 CE) 41
  Arcadius (383–408 CE) *134*
  Augustus (27 BCE–14 CE) *see* Augustus
  Aurelian (270–275 CE) *107*, 113
  Aurelius Antoninus (161–180 CE) *33*, 41, *41*

Caracalla (211–217 CE) 103, *103*, 104, *104*
Claudius (41–54 CE) 42, **54**, *64*
Commodus (180–192 CE) 41, 101, *102*
Constantine I (306–337 CE) *see* Constantine I
Constantius (305–306 CE) 118
Decius (249–251 CE) 117, 118
Diocletian (284–305 CE) *14*, 113–15, *114*, 118
Domitian (81–96 CE) 41, *45*
Galerius (305–311 CE) 118, *124*
Hadrian (117–138 CE) 41, 43, *43, 53*, 68, 90
Honorius (395–423 CE) *134*
Julian "the Apostate" (361–363 CE) 135–6, *135*
Justinian I (527–562 CE) *see* Justinian I
Maximinus (235–238 CE) 103
Nero (54–68 CE) 40
Nerva (96–98 CE) 41
Romulus Augustus (475–476 CE) 134, *147*
Septimius Severus (193–211 CE) 101, 103, 104, *104, 110*
Theodosius I (379–395 CE) 136, *136*, 137–40, *137*
Tiberius (14–37 CE) *6, 39*, 40, 45, *45*
Titus (79–81 CE) 69
Trajan (98–117 CE) 41, 42, 43, 68
Valerian (253–260 CE) 109, 118
Vespasian (69–79 CE) 40, *40*, **41**, *41*
Vitellius (69 CE) *40*
Roman Empire, the 6, 8, 12, *35*, **125**
  administration of 24–5, 27, 101–3
    Constantine's reforms of 119
    systems of 113–14, *125*
  amphitheatres in 58–9, *61*
  barbarian incursions into 107, 108–12, 129–33, *130*
  corruption in 104, 114, 135, 165
  cosmopolitan character of 47–8, *49*
  daily life in *16*, 58, **112**
  differentiation between West and East **125**, *126*
  Eastern Empire
    abundant revenues of 127
    architectural heritage of 164
    art of *163*, **163**
    Church and state and 126
    citizens of 165–6
    Justinian, emperor *see* Justinian
    religions of 166–8
    Western Church and 168–9
  eastern frontiers of 107–11, 129–33
  economy of *see* economic developments
  growth of 17–23, 24, 27, *35*, 41–3
  ideological crisis in 114–15
  imperial succession to
    adoption 41
    hereditary principle 41, 101
  internal unrest in 66–8, 101–3
  Justinian's attempts to restore **157**, 160–64, **160**
  political and cultural disintegration in 101
  road network of 47, 55
  sale of offices in 135, 165
  imperial cult in 63–5
  taxation *see* taxation
  trade in 69, 70, 109–10, *109*, 128
  Western Empire (4th–5th century CE)
    collapse of state apparatus in 127–34, 135
    division of Church and state in 126–7
Roman provinces 22, 24, 25
  Africa *see* Africa
  Asia Minor 22, 27, 125, *126*
  Britain (Britannia) 42, 125, 150–2
  Cisalpine Gaul 27
  Egypt 38, 123, 126
  Gaul *see* Gaul
  Judaea 76, 79

Mauretania 42
Moesia 111
Sicily and Sardinia 19, 22
Spain 21, 22
Syria *see* Syria
Transalpine Gaul 27
Roman religions
  Christianity and 119–22, 123
  civic authorities responsible for 62, **68**
  external influences on 65–6
  gods of 63, 65, **68**
  imperial cult (deification of emperor) 63–5, *64*, 68, 113–15
  mystery cults 66, 67, **68**
  pagan cults
    restoration of by Julian 135–6
    worship of forbidden by Theodosius 136–7
  sun-god cult 120, 121
  superstitions 63, 65, 92, 140–1
  temples 62, *62, 63*
  see also religions
Roman Republic, the
  Aegean hegemony 22
  agrarian reform in 29–30
  citizenship of 14, 15–16, 28, 29, 30, **33**, 47
  conscription and 17–18, 28
  constitution of 12–17, 25
  corruption in 25, 31, 32
  decline of 12–14, 27–36
  defeat of Carthage by 19, 23
  dictatorship in 30
  end of 32–6
  establishment of (509 BCE) **9**, 12
  foreign policy of **10**, 17
  Greek politics and 21–2
  Hellenization of 25–26
  naval warfare in 19, *21*
  plebeians (*plebs*) in 15–17, 30
  political structure of 12–17, 28, 31
  social foundations of 15–17
  territorial expansion of **10**, 17–23, *22, 23*
  Tribunes of the People in 16, 29
  votes for sale in 28
Romano-British civilization 150–52
Romans, the
  daily life of 58, **112**
  individual wealth of 24–5, *24*, 28, 29, 57–8
  social divisions of 55–7
Rome, city of 30, 58
  architectural ostentation in 54–5
  Caracalla Baths 59, *59*
  Colosseum 94
  daily life in 30, 58, **112**
  fortification of 107, *107*
  Forum 6, *36, 54*
    Curia Julia *14*
    Rostrum *15*
    Severus memorial arch *110*
    Trajan's Markets *112*
  mystic rituals banned in 67
  Ostrogoths expelled from 161
  Palatine Hill *45, 103*
  sacking of
    by Gauls (390 BCE) 18
    by Goths (410 CE) 132, 135, 145–6
    by Vandals (455 CE) 133
  site of on the Tiber 12
Rome, see of 173, 174
Rome (state)
  Christianity, reaction to in 87, 88–9
  coinage debased in 107
  education in 51, *51*
  Greek and Etruscan influences in 12, *13*, 26–7,

48–51, *52*
  inflation in 107, *107*, 135
  Jewish nationalism, response to in 89
  law in 27, *54*
  literature in 48–51, *50*
  provincial cities of 58, *59*
  public entertainments in 58–9, **60**, *92, 94*, 137
  technical skills in 54–5
  town-planning in 51, 54, 58, 59
  urban daily life in 58, **112**
  villas *see* villas
Romulus Augustus, last Western Roman emperor (475–476 CE) 134, *147*
Romulus and Remus, legendary founders of Rome 9, *9*
Rostrum (Roman Forum) *15*

S

Sadducees 80, 83
Samnite peoples 18, *18*
sarcophagi
  Christian *83, 84, 89, 90, 95, 117*
  of Constantina *120*
  Etruscan *10*
  Ludovisi *130*
  of Scipio family 22
Sassanid Dynasty in Persia
  Ardashir I and 108
  re-creation of Achaemenid Empire by 108–9, **109**
  Rome and 108–10
Saxons, Germanic peoples *24*, 129, 150
Scipio Aemilianus Africanus, Publius Cornelius (185–129 BCE), Roman general *19*
Scipio Africanus Major, Publius Cornelius (236–184 BCE), Roman general *20*
sculpture
  Etruscan *8, 9, 10*
  Greek *13, 26*
  Roman 27, 51
    Augustus, emperor *39, 40, 65*
    Boethius *155*
    Claudius, emperor *64*
    Commodus, emperor *102*
    Constantine, emperor *121*
    Greek influence on *13, 26*
    Hermes, Greek god *13*
    Julian the Apostate, emperor *135*
    Julius Caesar *32, 37*
    Ludovisi sarcophagus *130*
    Marcus Aurelius, emperor *41*
    Marius, general *31*
    Nero, emperor *91*
    sarcophagi *83, 84, 89, 90, 95, 117*
    Stilicho, general *134*
    Sulla, general *32*
    Vespasian, emperor *40*
    votive statues *12*
  Sassanid *111*
Seleucid Dynasty 21, 75, *75*, *121*
Senate 16, 24–5, 30, 32, 34, *54*
  conflict between emperor and 103
  Gracchi brothers and 29
  membership of 14–15, 47, *54*
  power of 40, 46, 103
  republican forms of 39, 101
serfdom, in later Roman Empire 106
Severus, Lucius Septimius (146–211 CE), Roman emperor (193–211 CE) 101, 103, 104, *104, 110*
  palace of *45, 103*

penetration into Mesopotamia by 108
worship of Egyptian gods under 65–6
Sicily, Roman conquest of 19, 21
Slav peoples 160, **160**, 164
slaves
  estate workers 28, 29, 61
  freedom for 61, *61*
  as labour for building 51, *52*
  ministri 65
  revolt of 66–8
  in Roman society 16, 28, 57, 61
Smyrna, persecution of Christians 93
Solomon's Temple
  first Temple 73, **78**
  second Temple 75, *75*
  third Temple 69, **78**, 89
  see also Jerusalem
Spain
  imperial government of 163
  as Roman province 21, 22
  as Vandal state 133, 156
  as Visigoth kingdom 156, **157**, 163, 176, *176*
Stephen (later St), apostle and first Christian
  martyr 85, 90
Stilicho, Flavius (d.408), Roman general of
  Vandal descent *134*
Stoicism *41*, 51
Suetonius Tranquillus, Roman historian **42**
Sulla, Lucius Cornelius (138–78 BCE), Roman
  general and politician 30–31, *32*, 42, 146
Symmachus, Quintus Aurelius (c.340–c.402 CE),
  Roman aristocrat 140
synagogues 74, 75, 77
  Dura-Europos *73, 121*
Syracuse 19, 21
Syria 72, 75, *75*
  Christianity in 118, 123, 126, 166–7
  communal monasticism in 170
  Huns in 134
  invasion of by Persia 109, **109**
  Monophysites 168
  as Roman province 79

T

Tabula Claudina **54**
Tacitus, Publius Cornelius (c.56–c.120 CE),
  Roman historian **41, 132**
taxation 24, 25, 27, 38, 46, 68–9
  avoidance of 128
  as cause of depopulation and urban
    decline 106–7
  decreasing base of 106, 114, 127–8, 133,
    135
  increasing levels of 104–7, 114
  Jewish resentment of 79
  reformation of by Constantine 119
  see also economic developments
Temple *see* Solomon's Temple
temples
  of Hadrian (Ephesus) *62*
  of Hercules Victor (Rome) *63*
  of the Palmyran gods (Dura-Europos) *75*
  of Vesta (Rome) *63*
Tertullian (c.152–222 CE) 117, 141
Thales of Miletus, philosopher 146
Theodelinda, queen of the Lombards *175*
Theodoric (455–526 CE), Ostrogothic king
  (474–526 CE) 154–6, *156*, 158, 160
Theodosius I (c.346–395 CE), Roman emperor in
  East (379–395 CE) 136, *136*, 137–40, *137*
  St Ambrose and 137–40

Thrace
  Bulgars in 164
  ravage of by Visigoths 132
Thuringians, Germanic peoples 129
Tiberius, Claudius Nero (42 BCE–37 CE),
  Roman emperor (14–37 CE) *6, 39*, 40
  palace of *45*, **45**
Titus Flavius Vespasianus (39–81 CE), Roman
  emperor (79–81 CE) 69
Toledo, Visigoth capital in Spain **157**, *176*
  see also Visigoths
Toulouse, Visigoth kingdom in Gaul 132–3,
  156, **157**, 158
trade 69, *70*, 128
  between Persia and Rome 109–10, **109**
Trajan (Marcus Ulpius Trajanus) (c.52–117 CE),
  Roman emperor (98–117 CE) 41, 42, 68
  conquest of Ctesiphon (Parthian capital) by 43
transport *30, 90, 113*
Twelve Caesars, The (Suetonius) **42**

U

urban decline 106–107, 135

V

Valens (c.328–378 CE), Eastern emperor
  (364–378 CE) 111, 132, *133*
Valerian (Publius Licinius Valerianus), Roman
  emperor (253–260 CE) 109
  murder of by Persians 118
  persecution of Christians by 118
Vandals, Germanic peoples *128*, 129, 132,
  133–4, 152
  conquest of North Africa by *128*, 133
  defeat of by Belisarius 161
  sacking of Rome by (455 CE) 133
Vespasian (Titus Flavius Vespasianus) (9–79 CE),
  Roman emperor (69–79 CE) 40, *40*, **41**
  murder of son (Domitian) by 41
Vesta, Roman household goddess *63*, **68**
Villanovan culture 11
villas *16, 49, 57, 60*, 104
  Boscoreale, Pompeii *51, 56, 105, 106*
  Villa of the Mysteries, Pompeii *67*
Virgil (Publius Vergilius Maro) (70–19 BCE),
  Roman poet 48, *50*
Visigoths, Germanic peoples 129–33, *133*, **157**
  conquest of by Franks 153
  conversion of to Christianity 176
  establishment of in Aquitaine 152, 158
  kingdom of (Spain) *132*, 156, 163
  kingdom of (Toulouse, Gaul) 132–3, 156,
    157, 158
  Vandals and 133
Vitelio, Aulus, Roman emperor (69 CE) **41**, *40*
Vitellius *see* Vitelio

W

wars
  civil (Roman) 30, 34, 38, 40, *40*, 101
  First Punic War (264–241 BCE) 18–19, **20**
  Judean (66–74 CE) **78**, 88
  with Mithridates 27
  Second Punic War (218–201 BCE) 19–21, *20*,
    20, *23*, 28
  Social War (90 BCE) 30
  Third Punic War (149–146 BCE) 23

see also battles
Western Empire
  collapse of 127–34, 135
  separation of from the East 113, 126–7
wine 69, *70*, 113
writing, Etruscan *10*

Z

Zealots, Jewish sect 80, 89
  Simon and 83
Zoroastrianism 66, 109

ACKNOWLEDGMENTS

PICTURE CREDITS
The publishers wish to thank the following for their kind permission to reproduce the illustrations in this book:

Key
b bottom; c centre; t top; l left; r right
AAA Ancient Art & Architecture Collection, London
ADO Agence Dagli Orti, Paris
AGE A.G.E. Fotostock, Barcelona
AISA Archivo Iconografico S.A., Barcelona
AKG AKG, London
BAL Bridgeman Art Library, London
BM British Museum, London
BN Bibliothèque Nationale, Paris
CP Catacombe di Priscilla, Rome
ET e.t. Archive, London
KM Kunsthistorisches Museum, Vienna
MAN Museo Arqueológico Nacional, Madrid
MANN Museo Archeologico Nazionale, Naples
MC Musei Capitolini, Rome
MGP Museo Gregoriano Profano, Vatican
MVG Museo di Villa Giulia, Rome
RHPL Robert Harding Picture Library, London
RMN Réunion des Musées Nationaux, Paris
SHP Sonia Halliday Photographs, Weston Turville, England
SK Studio Kopperman, Munich
V&A By courtesy of the trustees of the Victoria and Albert Museum, London
WFA Werner Forman Archive, London

Front cover: Michael Holford / BM
3 AISA
7 RHPL / Simon Harris
8 AKG / MC
9 AISA / MANN
10tl AISA / MVG
10b Jose Angel Gutiérrez
11 AKG / Tomb of Leopardi, Tarquinia
12 Jose Angel Gutiérrez
13 BAL / Archaeological Museum, Olympia
14 ADO
15 Scala
16t AISA / Museo Archeologico Nazionale, Venice
16b Corbis / Roger Wood
17 Scala
18tl RMN / Louvre, Paris
18r ET / MVG
19t Ny Carlsberg Glyptotek, Copenhagen
19b AGE
20t Scala / MC
21 AKG / Musei Pontificie, Vatican
22t Scala
22b AGE
23t AGE
23b RHPL / Robert Cundy
24–5t RMN / Louvre, Paris
24b BAL / BM

26 BAL / Giraudon / Louvre, Paris
27 Zardoya / Erich Lessing / Musée Granet, Aix-en-Provence
28t AISA / MC
28b Scala / MVG
29 Landesmuseum, Mainz
30 Zardoya / Erich Lessing / Maria Saal, Carinthia
31t ADO
31b BM
32t Scala / Museo Archeologico Nazionale, Venice
32b Jose Angel Gutiérrez
33 Scala / MC
34 Michael Holford
36 AISA
37 RHPL / Adam Woolfitt
38t BM
38c BM
39t KM
39b Oronoz / Musei Pontificie, Vatican
40t AISA
40cl AISA / MC
41 Zardoya / Erich Lessing
43 AGE
44tl RMN / H Lewandowski / Louvre, Paris
44r Fiorepress-Firo Foto
45 Oronoz
46 Stockmarket
47 AGE
48–9 ADO / Musée Archéologique de Sousse
50 AISA / Musée National du Bardo, Tunis
51t CM Dixon
51b Lauros-Giraudon / Landesmuseum, Trier
52b AGE
52t Scala / MGP
53 Axiom / James Morris
54 AISA / Museo della Civiltà Romana, Rome
56 AKG / Metropolitan Museum of Art, New York
57t AISA / MANN
57b AKG / Erich Lessing
58 AKG
59 Scala
60t AISA / Museo Archeologico, Taranto
60b Museo Arqueológico, Barcelona
61t Juan Avilés
61b Jürgen Liepe / Staatliche Museum, Berlin
62 AGE
63 Angelo Hornak
64 Scala / Museo Pio Clementino, Vatican
65t Scala / MGP
65b BM
66–7 AISA
68 Scala / Museo della Civiltà Romana, Rome
69t Scala
70 Scala / Museo Civico, Albega
71 BAL / Louvre, Paris
72 Scala / SS Cosma e Damiano, Rome
73 AKG / Erich Lessing / National Museum, Damascus
74t Werner Braun
74b Scala / Ipogeo di via Latina, Rome

75t BN
75b ADO / National Museum, Damascus
77 Scala / CP
78b AGE
79 Oronoz
80tl AISA / Museo Egizio, Turin
80b Zardoya / F Mayer
81 BAL / Battistero Neroniano, Ravenna
82 AAA / R Sheridan
83 Scala / S Prieto, Vatican
84 Iberpress / Giordano / S Ambrose, Milan
85t ET / S Costanza, Rome
85b Zardoya / Erich Lessing / Catacombe di S Domitilla, Rome
86 Scala / S Prieto, Vatican
89t Scala / Museo Pio Cristiano, Vatican
89b Scala / CP
90 AAA / Ronald Sheridan
91 Scala / Galleria degli Uffizi, Florence
92–3 Scala / Galleria Borghese, Rome
94t Scala / CP
94b AGE
95 Oronoz, Palazzo Rondanini, Rome
96-7 Scala / Catacombe di S Gennaro, Naples
99 BAL / Lambeth Palace Library, London (Ms.1370, f.115v)
100 Scala / Catacombe di S Ermete, Rome
102 AISA / MC
103t AISA / Xavier Navarro
103b Jürgen Liepe / Staatliche Museum, Berlin
104 AISA
105 Giraudon / BAL
106 AISA / Museo Archeologico Nazionale, Naples
107b Jose Angel Gutiérrez
107t MAN
108 AISA
110 AISA
111 Fiorepress-Firo Foto / S Fiore
112 Jose Angel Gutiérrez
113 AISA / Musée Calvet, Avignon
114 Scala / Biblioteca Apostolica, Vatican
115 BAL
116 SHP / Battistero degli Ariani, Ravenna
117 Scala / MGP
118 BAL / Private Collection
119 Bodleian Library, Oxford (Ms.378, f.84r)
120 Scala / S Costanza, Rome
121t AISA / MC
121b AAA / G Tortoli
122 AISA / Battistero degli Ariani, Ravenna
123t KM
123b Scala / Battistero degli Ariani, Ravenna
124t AAA
124b KM
127 RHPL
128 Giraudon / BAL / BM
129 BN
130–31 Scala / Museo delle Terme, Rome
132 MAN
133t KM
133b Bodleian Library, Oxford (Rol.159.2/83)
134 AISA

135 RMN / H Lewandowski / Louvre, Paris
136 AISA
137 Giraudon
138–9 ET / Mausolo di Galla Placidia, Ravenna
140 ADO / Musée National du Bardo, Tunis
141 Oronoz / Capilla S Vittore, Milan
142 Michael Holford / BM
143 Scala / S Lorenzo Maggiore, Milan
144 RHPL / F Jackson
145 Scala / Biblioteca Medicea Laurenziana, Florence (Ms.Plut.12; 17, f.3v)
146 Zardoya / Erich Lessing / Museo de Arcivescovado, Ravenna
147t BAL / Private Collection
147b Scala / Museo Civico de "Eta" Cristiana, Brescia
149 BAL / Biblioteca Medicea-Laurenziana, Florence (Ms.Plut.12.17, f.4r)
150 Michael Holford
151 Michael Holford
152 ET / Rheinisches Landesmuseum, Bonn
153 Lauros-Giraudon
154 BN
155 Giraudon
156l Iberpress
156r AGE
157 AISA
158 V&A / Ian Thomas
159 Scala / S Apollinare in Classe, Ravenna
161t Giraudon / Ainari / S Vitale, Ravenna
161b AISA / Museo Bargello, Florence
162 Zardoya / Erich Lessing / S Apollinare Nuovo, Ravenna
163 Scala / S Apollinare Nuovo, Ravenna
164 AISA
165 AISA
166 SHP / St Sozomenus, Galata, Cyprus
167 CM Dixon
168 Metropolitan Museum of Art, New York (Gift of George Blumenthal, 1941)
169 BAL / Louvre, Paris
170 Axiom / James Morris
171 AISA / S Costanza, Romes
172 Scala / Sacro Speco, Subiaco
173 BAL / Giraudon / Musée Condé, Chantilly
174 SHP / BN
175 Scala / Duomo, Monza
176 MAN
177 Trinity College Library, Dublin (Ms.57, f.21v)
179 Corpus Christi College, Cambridge (Ms.286, f.129v)

MAPS

Maps copyright © 1998 Debate page 109
Maps copyright © 1998 Helicon/Debate
pages 9, 20, 35, 55, 69, 88, 125, 126, 160

TEXT CREDITS

The publishers wish to thank the following
for their kind permission to reproduce the
translations and copyright material in this
book. Every effort has been made to trace
copyright owners, but if anyone has been
omitted we apologize and will, if informed,
make corrections in any future edition.

p.31 extract from *Fall of the Roman Republic:
Six Lives* by Plutarch, translated by Rex Warner
(Penguin Classics 1958) copyright © Rex
Warner, 1958. Reproduced by permission of
Penguin Books Ltd.; p.32 extract from *The
Conquest of Gaul* by Julius Caesar, translated
by S. A. Handford (Penguin Classics 1951) copy-
right © S. A. Handford, 1951. Reproduced by
permission of Penguin Books Ltd.; p.41 extract
from *The Histories* by Tacitus, translated by
Kenneth Wellesley (Penguin Classics 1964,
Revised edition 1975) copyright © 1964, 1972.
Reproduced by permission of Penguin Books
Ltd.; p.42 extract from *The Twelve Caesars* by
Suetonius, translated by Robert Graves, revised
by Michael Grant (Penguin Classics 1957,
Second revised edition 1979). Translation copyright © Robert Graves, 1957. Revised edition
copyright © Michael Grant Publications Ltd.,
1979. Reproduced by permission of A. P. Watt
Ltd. on behalf of the Robert Graves Copyright
Trust; p.58 extract from *Martial: Epigrams,
Vol. III* translated by D. R. Shackleton Bailey,
Cambridge, Mass., Harvard University Press,
1993. Reproduced by permission of the publishers
and the Loeb Classical Library; p.132 extract
from *The Agricola and the Germania* by Tacitus,
translated by H. Mattingly, revised by S. A.
Handford (Penguin Classics 1948, Revised
edition 1970) copyright © the Estate of
H. Mattingly, 1948, 1970 copyright © S. A.
Handford, 1970. Reproduced by permission
of Penguin Books Ltd.